This book is dedicated to everyone who has contributed to shaping my journey, brick by brick, with their unwavering support, listening ears, and empowering words. Your kindness, guidance, and encouragement have been the foundation of my growth. Each of you has played a vital role, proving that even the smallest gesture can have a profound impact on someone's life.

Thank you for being part of my story

Contents

Breaking In

Ultimate Playbook for Early Career Professionals

Harshani Samaradiwakara

Breaking In
Ultimate Playbook for Early Career Professionals

Finding my Path

When I was growing up, there was no electricity, no internet, and no mobile phones. We used kerosene lamps or candles to light our homes, and a simple torch to navigate the dark outdoors. The torch illuminated only a few steps ahead, leaving the rest of the path hidden in shadows, a fitting metaphor for how I saw my career back then: an uncertain journey with only faint glimpses of what lay ahead.

Each step I took was cautious and deliberate, guided by a hope that one day, the path would become clear. Along the way, I faced crossroads and encountered people who nudged me toward different routes, each promising its own possibilities. My guiding motivation was simple but powerful: the desire to make my parents proud and create a successful life. Yet, there were times I wondered if my definition of success was truly mine or shaped by others. Even so, I pressed forward, drawing strength from the encouragement of those around me.

Perhaps you feel the same way, unsure of what lies ahead and full of questions:

- "Which subjects should I choose for my A-levels?"
- "What kind of job should I aim for?"
- "Can I see myself in a corporate environment?"
- "If I study this, could I achieve my dream of becoming an architect?"
- "Is this the right job for me?"

As a teenager, I had countless questions but very few answers. Over time, I realised that some answers couldn't be found in books or from others; they had to come from within.

I once dreamed of becoming a doctor, imagining how proud it would make my parents. Despite my efforts, I didn't make it into medical school. Instead, I was offered a place to study agriculture, a subject connected to my roots as the child of a farmer. It wasn't my first choice, but it was my only chance for a free education. I decided to embrace it, moving seven hours away from home to live in a hostel. Still, I had no clear idea of who I wanted to become.

During university, I saw a friend choose a banking career instead of higher education. Her bold decision inspired me to explore other possibilities, and I began pursuing a professional qualification in Management Accounting alongside my degree. Money was tight, but I managed with a scholarship and determination. By my third year, I felt the need to earn my own income and started applying for jobs. After multiple attempts, I finally secured an entry-level position. Balancing work and studies was far more challenging than I had anticipated.

My first day at work was humbling. My supervisor, only slightly older but far more experienced, pointed out mistakes in a simple email I had written. I quickly realised I had much to learn, from photocopying and scheduling meetings to creating business presentations. Each skill I gained was a small but significant step toward becoming "career-ready."

As I progressed, I faced a deeper challenge: my job didn't align with my degree. Had I wasted four years of study? Uncertain, I applied for a management trainee position at a reputable bank. After a rigorous selection process, I was posted to a rural branch. It wasn't easy, but I saw it as a chance to grow.

Those early years taught me resilience and ignited a passion for mentoring others. I found joy in helping people clarify their goals and navigate their careers. Despite the demands of a growing family, I prioritised continuous learning, earning new qualifications, and stepping out of my comfort zone. My most significant growth came when I became the first female Business Development Manager at my bank, a role that pushed me to lead in uncharted territory. Over time, my path became clearer, and I discovered my true calling: empowering young talent to realise their potential.

That's when I decided to start my own venture, combining my passion and skills to guide others in achieving their dreams.

Looking back, I don't regret the time it took to find my path. Every challenge, detour, and success shaped the person I am today. This book is my way of sharing those lessons with you. It combines my experiences with insights from others I've met along the way, offering practical advice to help you find clarity and take confident steps toward your first job.

This is your journey, and I hope this book becomes a trusted companion, guiding you to embrace opportunities and make decisions that bring you closer to your goals.
Enjoy the journey, and remember, you're not alone.

Introduction

At some point, all of us will experience our first job, whether during school, after secondary education, or following graduation. Regardless of the role, the challenges we face in this journey are often similar.

Drawing from over 20 years in the corporate world as a banking and financial professional, as well as my experience as an academic in the UK, I've been deeply involved in recruitment, talent management, and mentoring individuals to achieve career success. My passion for enhancing employability led me to start the *Institute of Personal and Career Development (IPCD)*, where I continue to train, mentor, and expand my research into career development.

This book is a comprehensive guide to everything you need to know about job searching, applicable no matter where you live. Its content is based on my personal experiences, interviews with industry professionals from around the globe, extensive secondary research on the latest industry trends, and countless career conversations with people of all ages.

This book isn't just for reading, it's designed for action. The simple yet powerful exercises included will help you actively apply what you learn, equipping you with the skills and self-reflection needed to excel. Learning without application limits growth, but when you put these exercises into practice, you'll develop the tools necessary to succeed.

This book begins by identifying the challenges in the job market, followed by a focus on *self-awareness*, the foundation for understanding what career paths suit you best. By following the process outlined, you'll gain a deeper understanding of yourself, your strengths, and what drives you.

From there, the book explores how to research potential careers and teaches you to plan your career effectively using proven tools employed by leading career management professionals. You'll then learn how to craft an exceptional resume or Curriculum Vitae (CV) and write a standout cover letter using modern techniques designed to set you apart in today's competitive job market.

The journey doesn't end there. This book provides insights into following up strategically to increase your chances of getting shortlisted, building confidence for a variety of interview scenarios, and excelling under pressure. Finally, it guides you through negotiating job offers and stepping into your new role with the confidence of a seasoned professional.

The aim of this book is not just to help you land a job but to empower you to build a fulfilling career, one that aligns with your passions and enhances your overall happiness and success.

Don't forget to share this book with someone who might benefit from its guidance; it could be the key to transforming their life.

Employability Wheel

As you embark on your first career move or seek greater clarity as an early-career professional, it's essential to assess your understanding of key aspects of the job search and career development process. The "Employability Wheel" serves as a visual tool to help you evaluate where you currently stand and identify areas for improvement as you progress through this book.

Before diving into the chapters, take a moment to rate yourself on a scale of 1 to 10 for each criterion listed in Table 1 (1 = Strongly Disagree, 10 = Strongly Agree). This self-assessment will help you gauge your initial understanding and track your growth.

As you complete each chapter or finish reading the book, revisit the assessment and update your scores. If you score 7 or above in any area, it's a sign that you're ready to act and move forward with confidence.

If you feel you need additional support, remember, you're not alone. You can always reach out to me for guidance, just send me a message on LinkedIn.

No	Topic Area	Detailed Statements	Rating Now	Rating After
1	**The Future World of Work**	I understand the future skills in demand in the workplace and have started developing them.		
2	**Personal Mastery**	I know who I am and who I aspire to become.		
3	**Taking in charge of your Future**	I understand what it takes to effectively plan my career and know how to do it.		
4	**Personal Identity & Power Circle**	I know how to build my personal brand and grow my career network.		
5	**Golden Tools**	I am competent in creating a powerful CV/Resume, Cover Letter, and Statement of Purpose.		
6	**Turning Rejections to an Opportunity**	I can turn rejections into opportunities.		
7	**Interview Guide**	I can overcome my fears and face any interview with confidence		
8	**Thriving in your New Role**	. I can negotiate for the right offer and start my new job confidently.		

Graphically map your ratings here to visualise your understanding of employability skills.

According to the ratings you assigned colour each section to see a radar diagram of your own understanding of the world of work.

By doing this, you will appreciate your progress at the end of each chapter, which will positively impact your job search by allowing you to focus your efforts in the right areas.

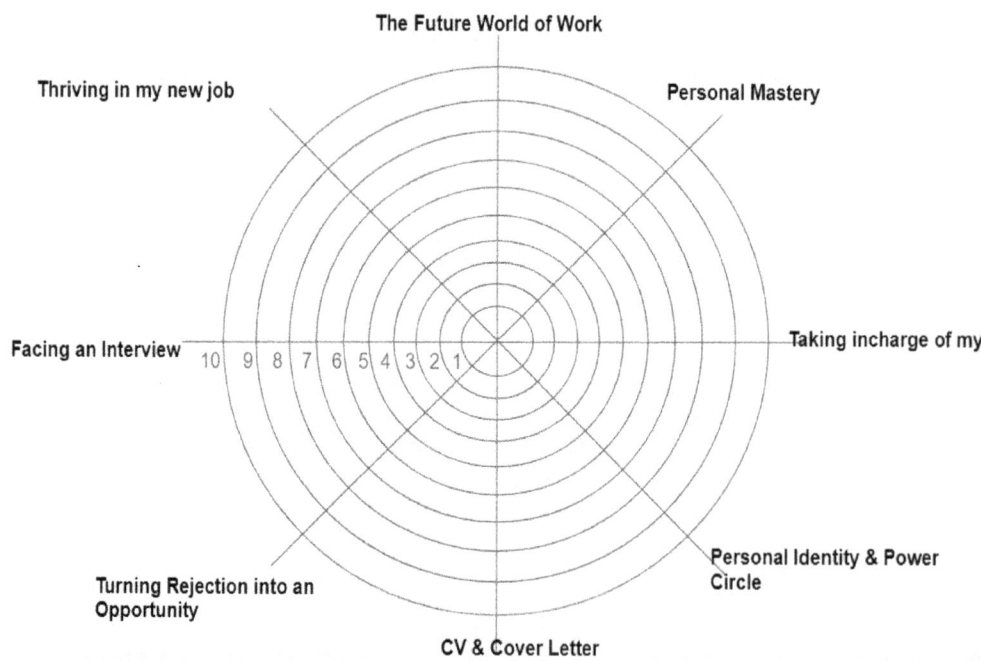

Figure 1 - My Employability Wheel

01

The Future World of Work

"A bend in the road is not the end of the road.
Unless you fail to make the turn"

— Helen Keller—

As an early-career professional, you are like a seedling emerging into the VUCA world. Your ability to adapt, stay resilient, and embrace change will determine your growth and success, helping you thrive in a dynamic environment.

At the end of reading this Chapter you will be able to:

- Identify why is landing the first job such a struggle.
- Understand the changing dynamics in the world of work.
- Identify ways to navigate this journey with confidence

Two Sides of the Coin

Landing the first job is often a challenge for many candidates, and this challenge can stem from both personal and external factors. When it comes to **employers' perspectives on first-time job seekers**, there are several common considerations they consider.

According to my research here are the three-key highlighted from **employers'** perspective.

Lacking Essential Skills

A recent survey by *Intelligent*, an online magazine focused on student life, revealed that 58% of U.S. managers and executives feel that graduates are not fully prepared for employment. Many employers report that new graduates often lack essential soft skills, such as effective communication, realistic salary expectations, and professional behaviour in interviews, all critical factors influencing hiring decisions.
The COVID-19 pandemic further interrupted the development of these skills, leaving some young professionals less prepared for workplace interactions. While unemployment rates among graduates have remained relatively low, sector mismatches are widening a gap in the job market. High-demand industries aren't always aligned with graduates' career interests, and desirable fields like tech have seen layoffs. This has led to a notable rise in underemployment, with the New York Federal Reserve reporting that 40% of 2023 graduates are working in roles below their skill levels.
Therefore, if you are a young career professional or undergraduate, you need to analyse your skill set with the industry demand in your sector. You will explore tools in Chapter 3 to analyse your skills GAP.

Low Retention Rates

According to a recent Gallup study on employee retention, half of U.S. employees are open to leaving their organisations. The 2024 *Achievers Engagement and Retention Report* further highlights that global employee engagement is critically low. In the U.S. and Canada, engagement levels hover around 31%, while other regions face even lower retention rates. Quiet quitting where 59% of employees worldwide are disengaged at work, continues to be an issue, especially for entry-level roles, where employees often seek better compensation and benefits elsewhere.

With rising inflation putting pressure on profit margins, companies are carefully managing their budgets. Many organisations are reducing training investments, focusing only on developing their permanent employees. This limited approach to training can hinder the growth and readiness of newer employees, impacting their long-term success and engagement.

Employers are highly focused on ensuring they get the best return on investment (ROI) when it comes to hiring, particularly for first-time job seekers. The talent management budget is a significant consideration for companies, and they want to ensure that the candidates they hire will contribute effectively to the organisation. As a result, they carefully assess candidates for a combination of the right skills, passion, and potential for growth.

To help early career professionals break through these barriers, **Chapter 6** of your book can explore **tools and strategies** that candidates can use to enhance their employability.

Increasingly Demanding Negotiations

The workplace is evolving in such a way that four generations now work within the same organisation. As a result, it has become increasingly challenging for employers to manage the varying expectations across all generations. Individuals also face the challenge of understanding these diverse perspectives and working cohesively.

Millennials and Gen Z have different expectations compared to previous generations. With a strong emphasis on work-life balance and job security, these younger generations are more assertive in negotiating for flexibility, competitive compensation, and benefits that align with their values and lifestyle. Companies are under growing pressure to meet these demands to attract and retain young talent.

In this book, you will explore these generational dynamics and learn how to negotiate your job offer effectively in such an environment, while creating a Win-Win scenario for both you and your potential employer in Chapter 6.

Let's explore the three key challenges from the **Candidate Perspective**.

Unclear about the Right Job

For teens, the vast number of career paths can be overwhelming, especially right after school when every field appears open yet uncertain. Entering an entry-level job too early can lead to a stagnant role without growth opportunities. Pursuing a degree can help focus options, allowing them to explore and specialise, yet the choice between academia and industry still presents multiple possibilities, making it difficult to commit. Further, as stated Jack Kelly in her article written to

Forbes referring the pulse survey results in 2023 highlighted that half of college graduates do not feel confident about their career prospects, with many feelings unprepared emotionally and professionally for the workforce.

On the other hand, the lifestyle of the current and upcoming generation of early career professionals are different to previous generations. Work packages are not designed to bring these differentiations, so that early careers struggling to choose the right job fit for their lifestyle.

You will learn valuable tools to effectively plan your career in Chapter 3 and can overcome this challenge.

Lack of Clarity on the Application Process

Even after identifying a dream job, the pathway to securing it can often seem unclear. Many roles, particularly niche or specialised positions, are not widely advertised. They are, often filled internally or through industry connections. Automatic rejections are a common experience, leading to frustration. To overcome this, learning how to approach recruiters, build a professional network, and leverage platforms like LinkedIn becomes crucial.

A major challenge for many candidates is the lack of basic skills in tailoring their CVs or job applications to specific opportunities. They struggle to make their CV stand out and often use the same generic version for every application. Additionally, different companies have varying recruitment processes, with each interview format presenting its own set of challenges. Even if candidates make it to the interview stage, they may not progress, leading to disappointment and frustration. This can sometimes trigger mental roadblocks that cause them to settle for less-than-ideal opportunities.

In Chapter 5, you will learn the tools and strategies to craft a resume that stands out and discover how to make the application process more effective.

Struggle to Stand Out from the Competition

A *Forbes* article highlighted that recent graduates often struggle to find decent jobs due to intense competition and employers' high expectations. Navigating through preliminary tests, selection exams, presentations, and multiple interview stages can be daunting. Successfully standing out requires more than just qualifications; it demands strategic self-presentation and resilience.

Many education systems do not prioritise career planning and skill development, although this is improving in developed countries. Schools and universities are gradually adopting career planning programs, but these are often limited in developing regions, leaving gaps in guidance. Access to mentorship and structured support is crucial in building the confidence needed for a successful career start.

In today's job market, even "entry-level" positions frequently require three to five years of experience, leaving many early career professionals unable to qualify. For those without prior internships or extracurricular achievements, building a competitive CV requires creative thinking. Participating in volunteer work, joining clubs, or taking on small projects can help highlight relevant skills and demonstrate a proactive attitude to potential employers.

This book provides all the answers and mentorship you need if you follow each chapter. You will learn the strategies to stand out, gain the required tools and support, and elevate yourself in the job market.

Even if you are a seasoned candidate with experience, these challenges remain, which you will explore through this book.

Now you know the two sides of the coin. Let's have a deep dive into the world of work.

The VUCA World

Are you worried about your future?
Are you curious about what could emerge tomorrow?
Are you anxious to see how you will cope with this change?
Do not worry! We all have those feelings despite an early career or seasoned professional. What we can do is understand and adapt to the changes and shape our journey.

When I was an undergraduate, I used to travel to the southern part of my beautiful island, Sri Lanka. My university, the University of Ruhuna, is renowned for both its quality of education and its unique architecture. Every week, I journeyed from Colombo, a trip that took more than four hours, offering a breathtaking view of the sea along the way.

The sea, ever-changing, seemed like a reflection of life itself. Some days, it was sunny and calm, its waters glistening in brilliant shades of blue. Other days, it was cloudy and rough, its mood subdued. On some occasions, it was turbulent and violent, a reminder of its untamed power. I often watched fishermen braving the waters, setting out to sea, their silhouettes vanishing on the horizon as they searched for their catch. These brave souls were vulnerable to the whims of nature, navigating the sea's unpredictable conditions and seizing its fleeting opportunities. Over time, their experience taught them to understand the waves and adapt to the sea's ever-changing temperament.

One unforgettable event etched this lesson deeply into my heart. On December 26, 2004, a devastating tsunami struck Sri Lanka. Many of my friends, colleagues, and their families lost their lives. It was a stark reminder of the sea's duality, its capacity for beauty and destruction.

The sea serves as a powerful metaphor for life. Like sailors braving the open ocean, we navigate the unpredictable waves of the world around us. The fears, uncertainties, and volatilities we face mirror the changing tides. Yet, as we sail through life, we learn, grow, and build resilience, much like the fishermen who adapt to the sea's rhythms.

This metaphor perfectly captures the essence of the VUCA (Volatility, Uncertainty, Complexity, Ambiguity) world we live in today. Just as sailors trust their instincts and hone their skills, we, too, must embrace faith, learning, and adaptability to thrive amidst life's challenges.

We Are Living in a VUCA World!

The concept of VUCA first introduced by the U.S. Army War College in 1987, stands for **Volatile, Uncertain, Complex, and Ambiguous**, four qualities that describe the fast-changing world we live in today. This is especially relevant for early career professionals as they enter a workforce marked by rapid shifts and evolving demands.

Why it is Volatile?

The world is evolving at an unprecedented pace. As a millennial, I witnessed a steady progression of digital growth during my youth, which allowed me ample time to adapt to new advancements. Today, however, technology evolves so rapidly that individual skills risk becoming obsolete within 3-5 years. In the blink of an eye, new knowledge emerges, reshaping industries and expectations.

Recently, we have experienced two distinct eras: before COVID and after COVID. The pandemic accelerated digital transformation, making workplaces more digital, flexible, and human-centred than ever before. We are increasingly witnessing the use of robots in hospitals, manufacturing processes, and care support, raising concerns about human skills being replaced by machines. Autonomous vehicles and drone technology have revolutionised transportation, turning childhood fantasies into reality. Understanding the potential for sudden disruptive changes and being prepared for such transitions is now more crucial than ever.

We all know that the world is evolving rapidly, but we can never predict what comes next. The environment around us is marked by significant volatility.

Why it is Uncertain?

The workplace is filled with uncertainty, driven by key trends that shape jobs and skill needs. According to the World Economic Forum's "Future of Jobs 2023" report, several factors will change how we work in the coming years:

a) Technology Adoption

Businesses rely on technology to stay competitive, and over 75% of companies plan to use big data, AI, digital platforms, and e-commerce. These technologies create opportunities for new roles but may replace some repetitive tasks. Staying updated on digital skills is crucial that cannot be replaced to remain competitive.

b) Green Transition

There is a global urgency to address climate change, driving a Green Transformation across industries as we rethink how we live and work. This transformation has three key dimensions: **social, environmental, and economic.**

- **Social**: Focuses on fostering a sustainable way of life by sharing resources, collaborating, and minimising disruptions within communities.
- **Environmental**: Emphasises reducing and eliminating harmful impacts on the environment through sustainable practices and innovation.

- **Economic**: Involves managing resources efficiently while maintaining profitability and supporting sustainable growth.

To achieve this transformation, two broad categories of skills are essential:
Technical Skills:

These include:
- **New skill sets** for emerging roles such as solar panel technicians, sustainable fashion designers, and drone operators. Jobs in renewable energy, sustainability, and environmental management are rapidly expanding, fuelled by daily innovations that reshape how we work.

- **Upgraded existing skills** in areas like sustainable farming, energy efficiency, and waste recycling to meet the evolving demands of traditional industries.

Transversal (Soft) Skills:
These encompass:
- **Disruptive thinking** to challenge conventional approaches.
- **Systems thinking** for understanding and addressing complex interdependencies.
- **Diversity, Equity, and Inclusion (DEI)** to foster collaboration across diverse teams.

A positive mindset toward sustainability and green practices is equally critical, as it opens doors to opportunities in these emerging fields and drives meaningful contributions to a sustainable future.

c) Skill Transformation

Analytical thinking, creativity, resilience, and technological skills are in high demand. With 44% of workers requiring reskilling, it's essential to evaluate your skills and identify any gaps to ensure you are prepared for the evolving job market.

In 2023, Kingston University, in collaboration with 2,000 business and industry leaders, 1,000 full-time students, 2,000 members of the wider public, and YouGov, published the Future Skills Report. The report highlights nine key attributes essential for the future workplace: creative problem-solving, digital competence, being enterprising, a questioning mindset, adaptability, empathy, collaboration, resilience, and self-awareness. Reflect on your abilities in these areas and assess whether you are truly "future-ready."

Additionally, recent industry studies emphasise that attitude and behaviour are among the most critical skills employers seek, as they require time and effort to develop. These include traits such as work ethic, politeness, attention to detail, honesty, integrity, adaptability, resilience, humility, empathy, and curiosity. Take a moment to reflect on these qualities and evaluate your understanding and personal strengths in these areas to better align with industry expectations.

d) Economic Pressures

Rising costs and slower economic growth are impacting job stability, particularly in manufacturing and supply chains. While some replaceable job tasks are being phased out, this shift also creates new opportunities. Many workers are transitioning to gig work and digital business models, leveraging their knowledge and skills to generate additional income outside their primary jobs.

Flexibility in work arrangements is becoming increasingly important, especially for managing work-life balance, such as childcare. However, the lifestyle expectations of younger generations, particularly Generation Alpha, often clash with existing salary structures, creating challenges for future employee retention.

Simultaneously, companies now have access to global talent through remote work arrangements and outsourcing. This trend significantly influences the earning potential and demand for the emerging workforce.

By understanding these economic pressures from both employer and employee perspectives, you can better prepare to navigate these uncertainties and position yourself for success in this evolving landscape.

Why it is complex?

Today's workplace is more complex due to intergenerational diversity and structural changes. A 23% shift in jobs is expected over the next five years. In the workplace, we now collaborate with people spanning four different generations, each bringing distinct perspectives and values. Soon, a significant shift will occur as Baby Boomers exit the workforce in what is often referred to as the "Silver Tsunami." This massive generational outflow will create gaps, not only in intellectual expertise but also in workplace attitudes, presenting younger generations with unprecedented opportunities to step into leadership roles.

Additionally, workplaces are becoming increasingly diverse, with employees hailing from multiple cultures and countries. These rapid changes, while unforeseen by many, are the result of long-term trends that we can trace and analyse.

To thrive in this ever-changing environment, we must cultivate the right mindset, one that embraces continuous learning and adaptability. Without this, we risk falling behind, unable to keep pace with the demands of a dynamic and interconnected world.

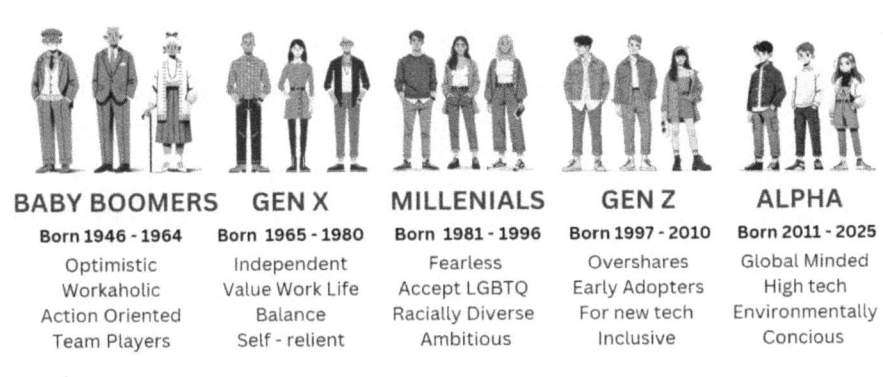

BABY BOOMERS	GEN X	MILLENIALS	GEN Z	ALPHA
Born 1946 - 1964	**Born 1965 - 1980**	**Born 1981 - 1996**	**Born 1997 - 2010**	**Born 2011 - 2025**
Optimistic	Independent	Fearless	Overshares	Global Minded
Workaholic	Value Work Life	Accept LGBTQ	Early Adopters	High tech
Action Oriented	Balance	Racially Diverse	For new tech	Environmentally
Team Players	Self - relient	Ambitious	Inclusive	Concious

Figure 2-Evolution of Generations

Why it is Ambiguous?

In this rapidly changing world, the future is often unclear. If you feel uncertain about your next steps, that's natural. Think of it like holding a torch: you can only see a little ahead, but by looking in different directions, you can gradually gain clarity.

Navigating ambiguity requires curiosity, faith, and support systems, like a compass and lighthouse for a ship's captain. By staying open to learning, adapting, and seeking guidance, you can create your own clear path forward. Embrace change, stay agile, and keep moving toward your goals.

In his TED Talk on Future Skills, Arndt Pechstein offers practical ways to navigate the VUCA world by providing solutions for each element:

Volatility: Managed through a Clear Vision

Without knowing the destination, boarding a bus could lead you astray. Similarly, setting a clear career vision is crucial to facing an unpredictable world. Having a strong purpose, your "why", is the foundation for building a clear vision and goal. (Chapter 3)

While careers used to follow a linear path, today they are more flexible, allowing for lateral moves across departments, companies, and even industries. Skills are often transferable, which means you can reach your goals by exploring new opportunities, even in the face of adversity. Creating a clear career plan can guide you toward growth. This plan should be dynamic; as you gain more experience, revisit and refine it to stay on track.

Uncertainty: Addressed through Upskilling

We often fall victim to "optimistic bias," overestimating our skills. In an ever-changing world, self-awareness is essential. As you read the next chapters, you will gain deeper insights into various aspects of your personal self to develop this clarity. Chapter 2 will guide you in analysing your skills gaps, providing a clear understanding of how to upskill for your future job role.

Recognising areas for improvement and committing to a cycle of learning, unlearning, and relearning is key to staying agile. Today, people tend to acquire specific skills rather than mastering entire roles. For example, to enhance your project management abilities, you could focus on creating effective project plans and using digital tools instead of completing a full certification. Targeted upskilling like this increases adaptability and helps you to perform well in your job. This will open up more job opportunities across various roles. Embracing curiosity and continuous learning is the most effective way to navigate uncertainty and thrive in a dynamic world.

Complexity: Tackled through Collaboration

Today's workplace requires collaboration across teams and departments, as working in isolation is no longer effective. Cross-functional teamwork fosters shared resources, skills, and knowledge, creating a unified workplace culture.

As an early career professional, aim to practice cooperation over competition, negotiate rather than bargain, and strive for win-win solutions in conflicts. Collaboration requires a shift in mindset and attitude toward openness and teamwork.

Ask yourself:
- How confident are you in teamwork?
- How do you contribute to team settings?
- Do you actively listen during group discussions?
- What challenges you faced while working in teams?
- How did you persuade and influence others in making decisions?

Reflecting on these questions will help you assess your readiness to navigate the complexity of a collaborative workplace. This helps you to identify potential training needs and gain knowledge in areas to improve yourself.

Ambiguity: Overcome through Agility

In an uncertain world, the future often seems foggy and unclear. As the saying goes, "To be the best tomorrow, be your best today."

Developing self-efficacy skills such as adaptability, resilience, and emotional intelligence will help you manage ambiguity. These skills enable you to understand and manage your emotions, adapt to new situations, and engage positively with others. Throughout your life journey experiences your face, work you undertaken, challenges you face shape these skills. However, having a better understanding and practice those learnings in your daily life expedites acquiring these skills.

As an early career professional, remember that rejections, failures, and criticisms are part of growth. Use these experiences to reflect, learn, and strengthen your journey. Resilience and a growth mindset will help you stand out in an ambiguous world.

Summary

As an early career professional, it's essential to recognise that simply *landing a job* doesn't mean you're truly ready for a career. To build a solid foundation, take the time to understand who you are and what you want to become. This self-awareness will help you create a clear career plan that aligns with your strengths and goals.

The job market is highly competitive and understanding why employers face challenges in recruiting can give you an edge. Knowing these "pain points" and common challenges that others encounter in finding the right job can set you apart from the competition.

Key strategies for success as an early-career professional include:
- **Having a Clear Vision**: Define your career goals and keep them in focus.
- **Upskilling**: Target skills that are in demand, especially those that are hard to automate.
- **Collaborative Work Skills**: Be prepared to work effectively with others and develop strong teamwork skills.
- **Resilience and Adaptability**: Build these qualities to navigate the inevitable ups and downs of career growth.

When planning, focus on skills that technology cannot easily replace, such as self-efficacy, collaboration, and ethical decision-making. Avoid roles with repetitive tasks, like clerical and basic administrative work, as these are more likely to be automated. Instead, emphasise building capabilities that add unique value to employers.

Reflective Activity: - Readiness check for future dynamics & Action Plan

Here's a self-assessment rating scale to help you reflect on your understanding of this chapter and track your progress.

Instructions: Read each statement and rate yourself from 1 to 10, where:

- 1 = Strongly Disagree
- 10 = Strongly Agree

If your score for any statement is below 7, consider actions you can take to improve in that area.

Areas concerned	Rating (1-10)
1.I have a clear vision of my career goals and understand the importance of career planning.	
2. I understand the competitive nature of the job market and what employers look for in early career professionals	
3. I know what skills are in demand and am actively working to upskill myself in those areas	
4. I am prepared to work collaboratively and have practised teamwork skills effectively.	
5. I am developing resilience and adaptability to navigate challenges in my early career.	
6. I focus on building skills that technology cannot easily replace, like self-efficacy, collaboration, and ethical decision-making.	
7. I recognise the limitations of roles with repetitive tasks and aim for roles that add unique value.	

Reflection: For any scores below 7, think about steps you can take to enhance your skills or understanding in that area. This could include additional learning, seeking feedback, or practising relevant skills.

02

Personal Mastery

"Awareness is the greatest agent for Change"

– Eckhart Tolle–

Like a seedling adapting to its environment, personal mastery is about understanding your strengths, emotions, and actions to navigate challenges. By nurturing self-awareness, discipline, and resilience, you create a strong foundation for growth. Mastering yourself empowers you to thrive and reach your full potential, even in the face of adversity

At the end of Reading this chapter You will be able to;

- Develop a better self-awareness to inform your decisions.
- Understand and gain more clarity about yourself and career journey.
- Develop effective goals and design a step-by-step action plan.

Who am I?

Self-awareness is the "conscious knowledge of one's own character, feelings, motives, and desires," according to Oxford Language. It is making you aware of "How you think", "How you feel" and "What you do".

The concept of the Johari Window is a tool that can help you reflect on your personal self, often compared to the iceberg metaphor. When you look at an iceberg, you only see the tip above the water, while a much larger portion remains hidden beneath the surface. Similarly, the world sees only your achievements and outward personality, but there is much more about you that remains unseen by others.

In this context, Johari identified four dimensions of your personal self. Understanding these dimensions can accelerate your personal growth and lead to a more fulfilling life. Let's explore each dimension in detail.

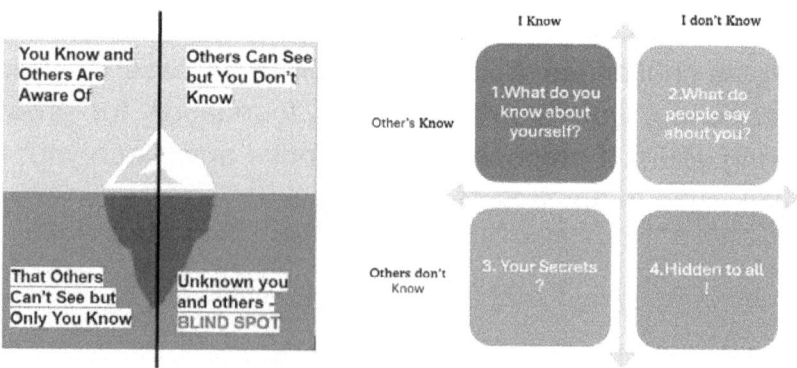

Figure 3-Iceberg vs Johari Window

1. Territories you know and others are also aware of:
With the prevalence of social media, much of our personal information is available to the outside world. Therefore, the world is aware of some parts of "You". However, there is often a gap between our true selves and the persona we project online. As a result, we may feel uncertain about our identity, even to the outside world.

2. Territories others can see but you don't know:
You look at the world with two eyes, but a thousand eyes are on you. Each of them views you through a different lens and provides feedback. This feedback can be positive, negative, or constructive. True positive or constructive feedback can help us discover hidden talents, motivate us to take action, and improve the way we do things. On the other hand, negative feedback can create self-doubt and often hinder our potential. Therefore, it is important to carefully filter and absorb only the feedback that supports our personal growth. Having strong self-awareness and surrounding ourselves with the right people allows us to seek valuable opinions and guidance.

3. Territories that others can't see but only you know:
These are the hidden territories within us, such as our thoughts, feelings, experiences, commitments, dreams and expectations etc. It's important to take time to reflect and remind us these territories and to compliment ourselves .When someone gives us feedback, always remind yourself that there are things that they do not know about you.

4. Territories that are unknown to both ends:
It is called as Blind Spot: Sometimes, we are not even aware of our own values, yearnings, or true selves. When we go through challenges or try new things, we uncover hidden blind spots. That's why continuously learning and exploring new experiences help us grow. To develop and better understand

ourselves, we need to open our minds and reflect on our experiences, especially during difficult times.

Our thoughts are like fireworks—we can only see them when they burst. However, before that explosion, they undergo a journey, gathering all the necessary ingredients along the way.

How can we find out about ourselves?
One powerful tool is reflecting on feedback

Use feedback from your colleagues, supervisors, friends, family, teachers, etc., both positive and negative, and think about the things you already knew about yourself. Place these under Category 1.

If there's something you never knew about yourself, put those comments under Category 2.

Next, reflect on the things you know about yourself but that others don't know, and categorise them as Category 3.

There are also instances where you find joy in doing something, but it often goes unnoticed. These are areas that may be hidden, also known as "blind spots." By staying open to new learning, you can uncover many more talents and capabilities that fall under blind spots.

During my life, I discovered many skills and aspects of myself by listening to others' feedback. Not all feedback is positive, but I didn't hold onto the negative. Instead, I reflected on why they expressed those thoughts and what I needed to improve. Do not be a sponge absorbing all feedback you get! Be a strainer that filter what is important to you.

If you treat feedback as a gift, it becomes the fast track to your success.

Congratulations! You did amazing.

Where am I?

Having a job doesn't necessarily mean you are career ready.

True career readiness comes from finding a role that aligns with your skills and provides opportunities for growth. Reflecting on my own experience, my first job was lucrative but not emotionally fulfilling or aligned with my skill set. Recognising this, I made the decision to seek a role that was a better fit. Once I became a banker, I thrived for 18 years in the same company, never considering a career change. Your job plays a crucial role in shaping your life, serving as a foundation for building satisfaction and fulfilment. Your career is something that you do to become who you want to be!. That's why it's vital to choose wisely.

Between the ages of 18 and 23, you're in a golden period, full of energy, hope, and a desire to learn. The experiences you gain during this time can significantly shape your future. With the right opportunities and exposure, you can accelerate your career journey. However, in today's fast-paced and ever-changing world, it's easy to feel uncertain. That's why it's important to focus on opportunities that offer lasting value. If you don't find the perfect fit immediately, don't be discouraged.

Take time each day to reflect, learn from your experiences, and prepare for future opportunities. From my journey, I've learned many lessons at different stages of life. These lessons can serve as tools to help you create your own career path more efficiently and with greater confidence. Let's dive in and explore more about who you are where are you and what you aim to achieve.

Imagine planting a seed. As it grows, it sends roots downward in search of water and nutrients to support its development, while the sprout reaches upward, seeking sunlight and space. Even if you plant two seeds in the same soil, with identical conditions, they won't grow the same way. This is because their growth is influenced not just by their environment but by their unique inner capabilities, such as Attitudes, Mindset, Values, Habits, Strengths, and Personality. This inner foundation, or "core," defines the direction and strength of their growth. The stronger the core, the more unstoppable the seed becomes.

Why is it circular? Because life is an iterative process of understanding, realisation, and evolution. Each core component contributes and plays a vital role in shaping your growth and progress.

The Core Wheel

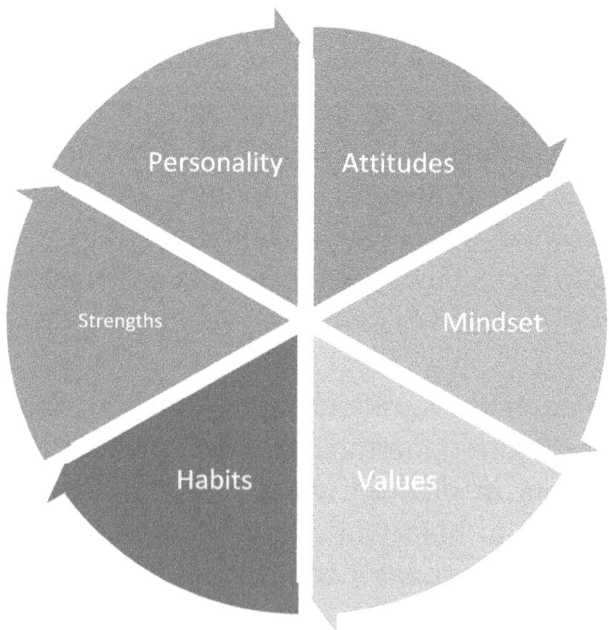

To understand where you are in your journey, you need to reflect on both your inner world (your core) and your outer environment. Let's start by exploring each aspects in depth.

Your Personality

Each of us is unique. Personality is influenced partly by our DNA, but largely by our environment. Your surroundings, including family, friends, upbringing, and the broader society, shape how you see and interact with the world. By recognising these influences, you can make conscious choices about who you want to be.

Historically, people associated personality traits with the elements of nature, Earth, Water, Fire, and Air each representing different qualities:
- **Earth**: Grounded, practical, reliable, and realistic
- **Water**: Creative, empathetic, nurturing, and intuitive
- **Fire**: Confident, passionate, independent, and brave
- **Air**: Witty, intellectual, social, and communicative

Think about how you might describe yourself. Do you feel more grounded like Earth, fluid and empathetic like Water, bold like Fire, or curious like Air? Or perhaps you're a blend of these qualities?

Your personality evolves with age, experiences, and the knowledge you gain. It is also fluid, adapting to different environments. Think about how you behave with friends and family compared to a public or professional setting—your thoughts, actions, and interactions change. Once you develop the capacity and skills to better understand your personality, you gain insight into the environments where you thrive.

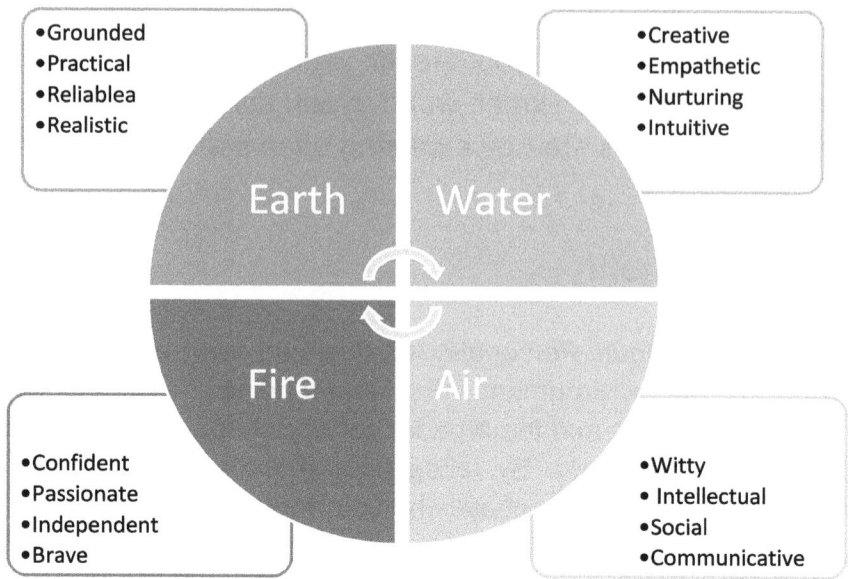

- Grounded
- Practical
- Reliablea
- Realistic

- Creative
- Empathetic
- Nurturing
- Intuitive

Earth Water

Fire Air

- Confident
- Passionate
- Independent
- Brave

- Witty
- Intellectual
- Social
- Communicative

Figure 4 -Simple elaboration of the types of Personalities

Let's dig deeper by discovering which aspects of your personality are most prominent.

Self-Discovery Exercises

1. **Take a Personality Test**

Online personality tests are a great starting point for gaining insights into your dominant traits. These tools analyse various aspects of your personality and provide a snapshot of your key qualities. By using one of these free tests, you can gain valuable self-awareness.

It's important to remember that no personality type is superior to another. The goal is not to label ourselves, but to understand our unique traits and make choices that align with them. Our personality can evolve over time, influenced by the context we are in, the different life stages we go through, and the experiences we encounter. As a result, it's essential to regularly engage in self-reflection to deepen our understanding of who we truly are.

Test type	How it explains different personality types
Big Five Personality Traits (OCEAN)	Measures five key dimensions: openness, conscientiousness, extraversion, agreeableness, and neuroticism.
Myers-Briggs Type Indicator (MBTI)	Categorises personality into 16 types based on preferences for introversion/extroversion, sensing/intuition, thinking/feeling, and judging/perceiving.
DISC Personality Assessment	Focuses on four behavioural styles: dominance, influence, steadiness, and conscientiousness.

Figure 5-List of common Personality tests

2. Ask People Close to You

Select five people who know you well, perhaps a parent, close friend, teacher, mentor, or colleague. Ask them the following questions to understand how they see you. Record their responses to identify patterns or common themes in their answers.

Questions	Person 1	Person 2	Person 3	Person 4	Person 5
1. How would you describe me in one word?					
2. What qualities do you value in me?					
3. What's the best experience you recall with me?					
4. What motivates me, in your view?					
5. What beliefs do I show in my actions?					
6. What am I naturally good at?					
7. Where do I seem to struggle?					
8. How do I work with others?					

Note: Feel free to adjust these questions. Starting with "What," "Why," "When," "Who," or "How" often leads to insightful answers.

Reflect on their answers. What patterns emerge? How do others describe your personality in one sentence? These findings will help you to discover not only personality, but many aspects of your life.

Are You Concerned About Your Personality?

Let me share an insight I gained from Susan Cain's book, *Quiet: The Power of Introverts in a World That Can't Stop Talking*. In her work, Cain argues that society exhibits a "cultural bias toward extroverts." Today, extroversion is often seen as a hallmark of success and is actively promoted.

Psychologist Robert McCrae further highlighted that personality traits, such as introversion and extroversion, are not evenly distributed worldwide. For example, lower levels of extroversion are found in East Asia compared to Western countries. As a result, Japanese and Chinese students studying in Western cultures are often misunderstood in team settings due to their quieter mannerisms.

Introversion vs. Extroversion

According to the book, *"The Success Code"* Written by John Lees clarify these two personality types, here's a comparative overview of his discussion.

Context	Introversion	Extroversion
Meeting People	Friendly and relaxed, but may prefer smaller gatherings	Energetic and independent, thrive in larger social settings
Social Contact	Interested in maintaining deep, meaningful connections	Prefer self-reliance, may avoid prolonged social interactions
Working with Teams	Prefer reflection and working independently	Draw energy from people and team collaboration
Approach to Actions	"Think-Do-Think" – deliberate and thoughtful in actions	"Do-Think-Do" – spontaneous and action-oriented
Decision-Making	Prudent and thoughtful	Spontaneous, lively, and occasionally impulsive
Talking About Self	Private and selective in sharing feelings	Open and expressive about emotions

Susan Cain further emphasises that introverts bring unique skills such as thoughtfulness, deep focus, and context-driven ideas, which add significant value in diverse settings. Those who fall between introversion and extroversion are considered **"ambiverts."**

Knowing where you fall on this scale can help you embrace your personality without worry or self-doubt. The key is to understand your tendencies and identify ways to interact with the world in a style that feels authentic.

Personality and Career Choices

We all display a mix of introvert and extrovert qualities, depending on the situation. These tendencies influence how we behave and adapt to our environment. For early-career individuals, self-doubt about personality often arises during interviews or when positioning oneself for a role.

Understanding your personality type is essential for mapping your skills to the right job and company. For example, if you're introverted, roles that require constant interaction, such as sales in a bank or insurance company, may not suit you. These roles demand energy from social interactions and a willingness to make new connections, which might feel draining for an introvert.

On the other hand, introverts might thrive in roles like creative design, back-office processes, software development, or accountancy, where they can focus on deep work and reflection. This self-awareness is crucial not only in selecting a job but also in how interviewers assess your fit for a role. They evaluate how well your personality aligns with the demands of the position.

Rather than trying to fit a societal ideal, focus on understanding your strengths and preferences. Use this awareness to choose environments where you can excel and feel comfortable.

In doing so, you'll unlock your potential and thrive in your career journey. Let's look at the DISC Personality types and according to the place you are in you can think about a potential career role.

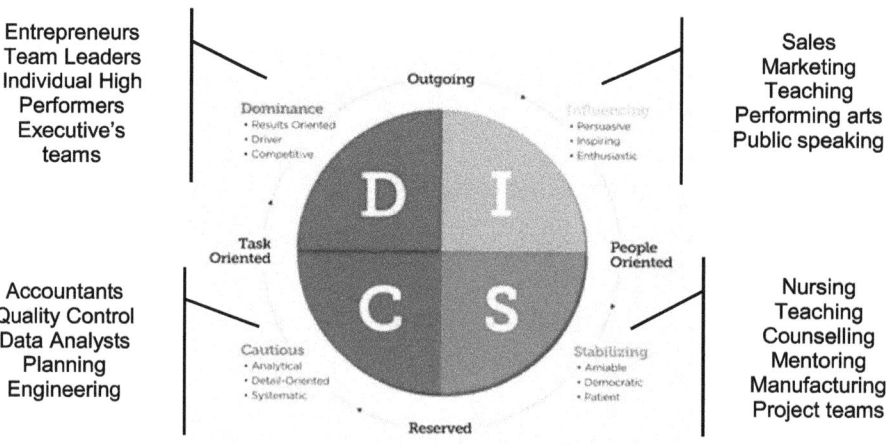

Figure 6 - DISC Personality type and Potential Job Role

Let's look at a potential interview scenario.

During an interview, the pressure to showcase your experience, industry knowledge, and the thoughtful questions you have about the business can sometimes cause you to overlook the importance of your personality. While competency-based or hypothetical questions may cause you to stress about providing the "perfect" answer, always remember that it's you as a person they are hiring. If your personality doesn't align with the company's culture, you likely won't be happy there anyway.

So, if you're a fun, friendly, and caring person, let that shine through. If you love helping others learn, share that passion; if you're adaptable and willing to take on any challenge, provide examples in response to questions like "Tell me about yourself." If you're someone who thinks differently or excels at inspiring creativity in others, share those experiences too.

Before applying for jobs or heading into an interview, take time to reflect on who you are. Ask your friends what they appreciate about you and consider your strengths and how you stand out. A personality test can also provide valuable insights into your strengths and areas for growth, helping you clarify what you're truly good at.

Recognise the unique traits that make you a valuable asset to any team and ensure those qualities shine when meeting with a hiring manager.

Your Values

Your beliefs and attitudes shape your values, which bring clarity to what matters most to you in life. Identifying these values is crucial, especially when starting your career. They not only guide your actions and decisions but also help you connect with the right employers and roles.

Let's go through a step-by-step journey to help you discover and understand your core values. By the end, you'll have a clearer picture of who you are and what you stand for, an invaluable asset when applying for your first job.

Why Are Values Important?

Values are the qualities and principles that drive our behaviours and attitudes. For instance, if you value "integrity," you'll prioritise honesty in your interactions and seek to work with people who also uphold integrity.

Knowing your values allows you to:
- Align with the right companies and roles where your values resonate with their mission and culture.
- Showcase your values in interviews by sharing experiences that highlight them.
- Stay true to yourself in your career, making it easier to find satisfaction and purpose in your work.

When you apply for a job, explore the company's values. Do they align with yours? Understanding this can help you choose an environment where you can thrive and feel fulfilled.

Value Discovery Tool

Reflect on these questions to begin identifying your values:

1. **How do you work with others**

Think about the **qualities you bring** to a team.

Examples: Committed, team-oriented, collaborative, friendly, supportive, etc. List values you demonstrate when working with others.

2. **What do you expect from others**

Consider the **qualities you admire** and expect in colleagues.
Examples: Honesty, accountability, respect, authenticity, integrity, kindness, empathy.
List values you seek in others, which reflect what you value yourself.

3. **How do you feel when taking action**

Reflect on **how you feel** when engaging with your work.
Examples: Passionate, determined, motivated, enthusiastic.
List values that describe how you feel when you're fully engaged in something.

4. **What do you expect in work done by others**

Think about **qualities you think** in completed tasks or projects.
Examples: Ethical, loyal, patient, organised, detail oriented.
List values you think are important when assessing work.

Activity: Identifying Your Core Values

1. Reflect on Previous Exercises

Consider answers you've received about yourself, especially from any recent self-discovery exercises.

2. List Your Values
   Write down responses in each category:
   ○ Values You Demonstrate
   ○ Values You Expect
   ○ Values You Feel
   ○ Values You Think

Values You Demonstrate	Values You Expect	Values That feel	Values You Think

3. **Explore the Value List**
   Review a broader list given below of values for inspiration. Take your time and brainstorm more values. Highlight the values that closely align with you.

Accountability	Balanced	Dedication	Innovative	Friendly
Achievement	Courage	Empathy	Loyal	Honest
Autonomy	Commitment	Passionate	Love	Responsive
Affection	Caring	Unique	Open	Patience
Authenticity	Competent	Dedicated	Passionate	Sustainable
Professional	Compassion	Funny	Enthusiastic	Ethical
Trusted	Curiosity	Responsible	Peaceful	Kind
Teamwork	Creative	Respect	Graceful	Spiritual
Forgiveness	Gratitude	Quality	Safety	Faithful
Fame	Persevere	Stability	Risk Taking	Joyful
Competent	Determined	Variety	Harmony	Inclusive
Excellence	Challenging	Stewardship	Strength	Empowerment

Figure 7 - Example Value List

4. Highlight Your Top 10
Narrow down your list to ten values that resonate most with you.

5. Identify Your Top 5
Reflect on these ten values, then reduce the list to your top five.

6. Select Your Core 3
Finally, pick the three core values that feel most aligned with who you are. These should represent the essence of your identity.

Applying Your Values to Your Job Search

Now that you've identified your core values, use them as a guide in your job search:

- Research Company Values: Look up the company's mission, vision, and core values. Do they match or support your own? This alignment will help you feel a greater connection to your work.

- Align Your Experiences: When crafting your resume or preparing for interviews, think of examples from your past experiences (school projects, volunteer work, hobbies) that showcase these values. Employers appreciate candidates who bring a clear sense of purpose and integrity.

- Bring Clarity to Your Identity: Your values are foundational to your personal brand. They will influence how you make decisions, interact with others, and navigate challenges. Building your career around these core values will keep you grounded and motivated.

Why This Matters for Candidates

Values aren't just buzzwords, they are the foundation of your professional identity. By defining your values early on, you'll have a strong sense of self as you embark on your career. It will guide you in making choices that feel right, help you stand out to employers, and ultimately lead you to a fulfilling path.

When you understand your values and actively pursue them in your work, you're more likely to succeed and find joy in what you do.

When you live true to your values, it demonstrates through your behaviour and creates a unique identity around you. The people who interview you, supervise you, and work with you start to understand you better. Therefore, the values you uphold are crucial to thriving in any environment.

As you work, you will get inspiration from the people around you and develop new values. Therefore, it is also important to consider where you work and with whom you work. Take the time to define your values and let them be your compass in your job search and beyond.

Your Attitude

The word "attitude" originates from the Latin word *aptus*, meaning "fitness" or "adaptiveness." This highlights an essential quality of attitudes: they are adaptive responses to our surroundings. According to research by Barbra (1978) on the relationship between attitude and behaviour, attitude is defined as a subjective or mental state in preparation for action. In other words, it is our mindset and readiness to react to the world around us.

Philosopher Herbert Spencer emphasised that the attitude of our mind impacts the way we judge situations and make decisions. Essentially, attitude is an integral part of our **personality**. It reflects our mindset and influences our outlook on life, our reactions, and even our long-term behaviour.

Beliefs vs Attitudes

Beliefs are different from attitudes, yet they play a critical role in how we see the world. A belief is a state of mind or conviction that we hold to be true, even if we lack direct evidence or proof. It's the acceptance of an idea, statement, or proposition as true or valid. Beliefs can be influenced by many factors, such as religion, culture, and personal experience, and can range from simple ideas to deeply ingrained convictions.

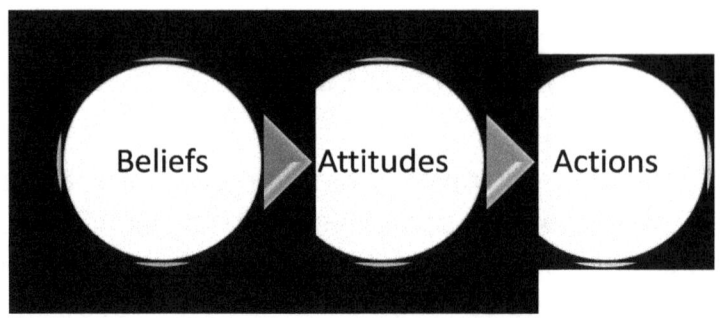

What we believe shapes our perceptions. For instance, what you see in a picture can be influenced by your beliefs; they act as lenses that colour your perception, defining your attitudes, behaviours, opinions, and actions. Therefore, if you want to change your actions, you must start by examining and potentially changing your beliefs. This process requires a strong sense of purpose, clear reasoning, and a supportive environment.

If you look at the picture below, it illustrates how values, attitudes, beliefs, and actions combine, using the analogy of a tree.

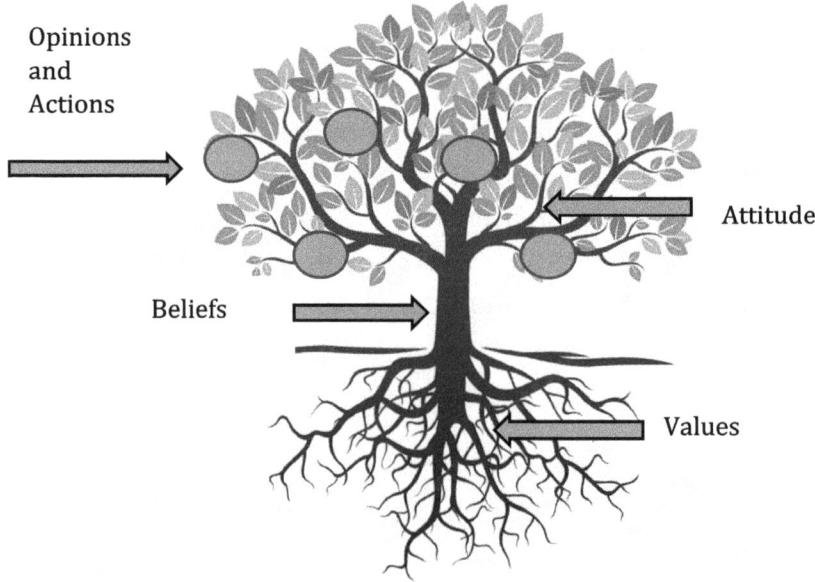

- **Values are the roots**:
  They define our identity and form the foundation of our character. Strong values anchor us, much like deep roots provide stability to a tree. The deeper your values, the stronger your core becomes.

- **Beliefs stem from your environment**:
  Our surroundings shape our beliefs, which in turn shape who we are and contribute to forming our identity. Beliefs are the trunk, providing structure and support as we grow. Size, Strength and texture influenced by the inheritance, environment and the way it gets nurtured.

- **Attitudes are the branches**:
  They represent how we bend, adapt, and expand while navigating through life. Our attitudes extend from our beliefs, influencing how we approach challenges and opportunities.

- **Actions are the leaves and fruits**:
  These are the visible outcomes of our values, beliefs, and attitudes. They are what others see and interact with, reflecting the essence of who we are.

This analogy highlights a profound truth: **what you sow, you will harvest**. The stronger your roots (values), the healthier your tree (identity and actions) will be. This interconnected system reminds us that cultivating positive values and beliefs can lead to growth that is both meaningful and impactful.

Attitudes, Beliefs and Behaviour

Attitudes are not fixed; they are shaped by our interactions with people and our environment over time. As we experience life, certain attitudes become "programmed," turning into habits. Others might even refer to these ingrained attitudes as our **habits** because they become automatic responses to familiar situations.

Humans are naturally impulsive and spontaneous. When we encounter a new situation, we instinctively refer to past experiences, using our stored responses as guides to evaluate the present. Research confirms that attitudes are often spontaneous reactions to environmental cues. Since attitudes can form and evolve through experiences, they can be changed. This means that by consciously adjusting our experiences, we can reshape our attitudes and, ultimately, our behaviour.

The environment you are in greatly influences your beliefs, attitudes, and behaviours, which consequently shape your actions.

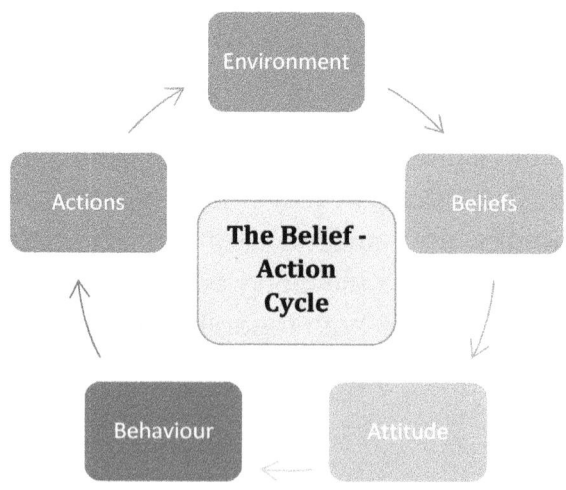

Reflecting on Your Beliefs and Attitudes

Let's take a moment to revisit the self-discovery exercise you completed with your five selected "cheerleaders" ; the people whose opinions you value most. Think about their responses and reflect on how your beliefs might have shaped your past decisions and actions. Consider the following prompts:

1. **How have your beliefs influenced your decisions?**
2. **Do you have any contradictory beliefs about certain topics?** How were these beliefs formed?
3. **What recent actions have you taken that you now question or regret?** What beliefs and attitudes influenced those actions?
4. **How can you change any beliefs that led to negative outcomes?** What new actions can you take?

Having an open mind and engaging in these reflective thoughts will help you develop a better understanding of yourself. This self-awareness will bring clarity to your journey.

Example: Reflecting on the Belief around working overtime

Let's look at an example to illustrate this reflective process:
Question: *What do you think about working overtime? Is it good or bad?*

1. **What shapes your view on this?** Have past experiences, family influences, or personal incidents shaped your belief?
   You might recall how you feel when your farther work overtime and you having less time to be with him Or You recall how your brother climbed up the ladder fast and delivered successful projects and celebrated those.

2. **How would you react if your supervisor asked you to work over the weekend to complete a project?**
Your answer is shaped by the experience and belief that you had, and your action or response shows what it is to the world.

3. **If your employer informed you that your role would include night shifts or on-call rotations, would you accept the job?**

Reflecting on these questions can help you trace your attitudes back to underlying beliefs. By identifying these beliefs, you can explore their origins, consider other perspectives, and decide whether they still serve you well. This process brings clarity to your thoughts, allowing you to align your actions more closely with your goals and values.

Moving Forward with Self-Discovery

By examining your beliefs, attitudes, and responses, you're gaining valuable insight into your **inner self**. This awareness can help you make conscious choices that align with your goals and improve your interactions with others. Remember, self-discovery is a continuous journey. Reflect on your experiences, keep an open mind, and be willing to adapt as you grow.

This chapter encourages you to ask questions, challenge assumptions, and embrace new perspectives. Through this reflective practice, you're not only gaining clarity about who you are but also developing a deeper understanding of how you interact with the world. This awareness is a powerful tool that will guide you through future challenges, enabling you to make choices that align with your values and purpose.

Your Mindset

In simple terms, a mindset refers to how we think about and approach different situations in life. It is a **set of** attitudes, beliefs, and assumptions that shape our behaviours and reactions.

Imagine you're about to start your first job. You've studied, practised, and are ready to dive into the workforce. But here's a surprising truth: your *mindset* could be one of the most important factors in your success. Let's explore the difference between the two key mindsets highlighted by a world-renowned psychologist ,Carol Dwek in her book "Mindset" and see where you might fit in.

Where Do You Belong? Fixed or Growth?

Take a moment to find out. Answer "Yes" or "No" to these statements:
1. When you become an adult, it's very difficult to change your abilities.
2. You are born with talents that cannot change.
3. You have a certain intelligence level that is unchangeable.
4. It's hard to learn new skills.
5. You can improve your ability by taking small steps.
6. Your intelligence is within your control.
7. Your natural talent can improve with practice.
8. You can always learn new skills at any age.

If you said "Yes" to statements 1-4, you might have a *Fixed Mindset*. If you said "Yes" to statements 5-8, you lean toward a *Growth Mindset*. If your answers are mixed, you may have a blend of both.

The Fixed Mindset

People with a fixed mindset believe that abilities are set in stone. Intelligence, talent, and skills are seen as unchangeable. Success depends on what you're born with, not what you can improve.

Example: Pete, a bright young man, performed well in school and entered university to study Data Science. But Pete believed he wasn't good at math, so he avoided it. Instead of pushing through his struggles, he switched subjects, convinced it was too late to improve. This fixed mindset impacted his confidence and left him feeling stuck and embarrassed.

Reflection: Have you ever felt you weren't "good enough" at something? Maybe math, public speaking, or sports? Or perhaps you've seen a friend give up because they didn't think they could improve?

In relationships, people with fixed mindsets might walk away when things get tough. In business, they struggle to face challenges. And in sports, they quit after one bad game, thinking they're just not cut out for it. A fixed mindset keeps them from embracing growth opportunities.

The Growth Mindset

People with a growth mindset believe that with effort and perseverance, they can improve and develop new skills. They embrace challenges, learn from mistakes, and see setbacks as steps on the path to success.

Example: Imagine a young woman, Sarah, who struggled with presentations. Instead of saying, "I'm just not a good speaker," she practised, asked for feedback, and took every opportunity to improve. Now, she confidently leads team meetings and continues to challenge herself in new areas.

Reflection: Do you have areas where you want to improve? A growth mindset can help you reach your potential by viewing challenges as learning experiences.

Embracing a Growth Mindset: Key Strategies

Transforming from a Fixed Mindset to a Growth Mindset takes practice, but it's possible! Here's how:

1. **Acknowledge Imperfection**
   Action: See imperfections as opportunities.
   Strategy: Reflect on areas where you feel inadequate and view them as starting points for growth.

2. **View Challenges as Opportunities**
   Action: Reframe challenges as chances to learn.
   Strategy: Ask, "What can I learn from this?" when facing difficulties.

3. **Shift "Failure" to "Learning"**
   Action: See failure as a learning experience.
   Strategy: After setbacks, assess what went wrong and how to improve.

4. **Cultivate Purpose**
   Action: Align your goals with your values.
   Strategy: Reflect on how your goals connect to your long-term vision.

5. **Use "Yet" to Unlock Potential**
   Action: Add "yet" to your vocabulary.
   Strategy: Instead of "I can't do this," say "I can't do this yet."

6. **Learn from Feedback**
   Action: Value constructive feedback.
   Strategy: Seek feedback from mentors and peers to fuel improvement.

7. **Celebrate Effort, Not Just Results**
   Action: Focus on the process, not just the outcome.
   Strategy: Acknowledge your effort and dedication to stay motivated.

8. **Reflect on Learning**
   Action: Review your growth regularly.
   Strategy: Keep a journal of your learning experiences.

9. **Set Learning Goals**
   Action: Focus on growth, not just performance.
   Strategy: Set goals that push you to develop new skills.

10. **Be Curious**
    Action: Approach tasks with curiosity and a desire to learn.

Role of Mindset in Career World

In her book *Mindset*, Dr. Carol Dweck describes how mindset can be shaped by praise. In a study with students, one group was praised for intelligence ("You're so smart!"), while the other was praised for effort ("You worked hard!"). When faced with harder tasks, the "smart" group shied away, while the "hard work" group embraced the challenge.

As you step into your career, recognise the power of growth-minded thinking.

Choose to focus on effort over innate ability, and you'll unlock your potential.

When you find a good job opportunity that align with your knowledge areas, approach those and apply. Challenge yourself to learn additional skills that you need to develop.

This highlighted another important aspect of how you provide feedback to other. Always praise focused on their commitment which will enable growth mindset and foster others to contribute and perform more. This is important in creating a positive working culture.

One important factor contributing to this is **self-image**. How you think about yourself is reflected in your actions. We all have both a growth and a fixed mindset, depending on the context. By cultivating a "can-do" mindset, you can change the way you view yourself, which in turn can transform your actions and behaviours. This brings significant value to the self you present to the world and shapes how others perceive you. When your self-perception aligns with how others perceive you, you can thrive in your authentic self. This alignment is crucial for self-awareness and personal growth.

Your Strengths

Why Strength Matters?

From a young age, we're often encouraged to focus on our weaknesses, to "improve" and "fix" them. But after years of trying, how successful has that approach really been? Imagine if, instead, you'd spent all that time building on your natural strengths, your unique abilities and qualities. You would be honing the skills that come more naturally to you, making progress faster and achieving a greater sense of confidence and satisfaction.

If you look at people who've achieved their goals, you'll notice they often focus on what they're *good at.* This is where many young individuals get stuck, too. Rather than fixating on weaknesses, successful people leverage their strengths to stand out and succeed. Let's explore how you can identify your own strengths and use them to reach your career goals.

The Five Strength Clues

Think about a time when you felt truly at your best, using your strengths. Revisit those experiences in detail to uncover what makes you unique.
1. **Where were you?**
2. **Who or what else was there?**
3. **What was your strength that you made use of?**
4. **What Impact did it bring?**
5. **How did you feel while using your strengths?**
6. **How did you feel afterwards?**

Reflecting on these questions will help you recognise the moments when you've been fully engaged and effective. It will also help you identify the types of situations, tasks, and people that bring out the best in you.

Early in my career as a Project Executive at the bank, I was given a challenging task—not to manage an existing client portfolio, but to build my own from scratch. At first, I couldn't even imagine how I would accomplish this. However, I explored every possible way to reach out to new clients, and eventually, I secured my first one.

I went to meet the client with my manager, only to find that they were highly demanding, seeking a clear differentiator in our proposal. To prepare, I thoroughly researched their specific needs, reached out to a few employees for insights, and obtained references. I then drafted a detailed proposal that compared our offerings with other banks, highlighting what made our solution stand out.

My *never-give-up* attitude and preparation were key. I always challenge myself to turn rejections into acceptances, so I made sure the proposal addressed every demand. The client was impressed—it exceeded their expectations, and they couldn't say no. I won my first client, and as I walked out of their office, I felt like a true winner. That moment filled me with a deep sense of accomplishment and confidence.

Through this experience, I realized that working with people and creating new business are my *superpowers*. That fuelled by my values of "Commitment", "Positivity", "Caring" and being Empathetic". It gave me the courage to continue reaching out to new clients, and over the years, I grew my portfolio from millions to billions.

This experience illustrates the power of playing to your strengths. When you focus on what you do best, it builds momentum and opens doors to greater success. Like everyone, I have weaknesses, but by prioritising my strengths, I've found that they naturally help me improve in other areas over time.

The Formula for Success

What exactly does "Strength" mean.

Strengths have three main elements:

Gifts: Natural talents you're born with, like creativity, communication, or analytical thinking. Imagine these talents as unpolished gems; they're valuable on their own, but if you invest in developing them, they'll shine even brighter.

Passions (What You Love): The activities you genuinely enjoy when money is not your priority. These could be adventurous pursuits, hobbies, or activities you do without needing any external motivation. Passionate interests help you build skills naturally over time.

Knowledge and Skills: The abilities you develop through learning and experience, whether in school, through courses, or life experiences. The more you invest in building knowledge in areas that align with your gifts and passions, the more empowered you become.

All the above components have a multiplying effect on your strengths.

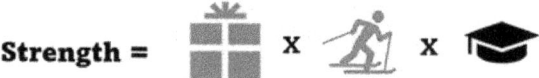

Gifts x Passions x Knowledge and Skills.

When you focus on developing your talents, acquiring new skills, and expanding your knowledge, your strengths grow exponentially. When these areas interconnect, they create a ripple effect, amplifying your overall capabilities and impact. Therefore, I call it as my "Formula for Success".

How to Transform Through Strengths

When you focus on weaknesses, your mindset often becomes negative. You might start to compare yourself to others, feel discouraged, or give up quickly. But when you work from a place of strength, using your talents, passions, and knowledge, you build a strong foundation for growth. Most people have strengths but may not be using them effectively. Success lies in organising and aligning your strengths to unleash your potential and make continuous progress.

Here are some strategies to help you get started:

1. Manage Self-Sabotage

Self-sabotage often manifests as negative self-talk and mental blocks that hinder your progress. These might include thoughts like, *"I can't do this," "It has to be perfect,"* or *"I'm not good enough."* Our brains are wired for *fight, flight, or freeze* in stressful situations, which can reinforce these patterns. When self-sabotaging thoughts dominate, they trap us in repetitive and limiting beliefs.

To overcome self-sabotaging thoughts, practice mindfulness and actively recognise negative patterns. Challenge your inner critic by replacing harmful dialogue with positive affirmations.

Begin each day with uplifting self-talk, focusing on your strengths and affirming that things will work out in your favour. Adopting a "SAGE mindset," which views every challenge as an opportunity for growth, helps shift mental patterns toward empowerment and positivity.

Robin Sharma's book *Who Will Cry When You Die* emphasises the power of postponing worry time. I've personally applied this technique in my professional life. Whenever I noticed my mind engaging in negative self-talk, I would consciously tell myself to revisit those worries after work at 7 p.m. This allowed me to focus on the task at hand, and over time, I became more effective at managing my mental saboteurs and by the time I got to 7 p.m. the urge to worry disappeared.

Before attending an interview, starting college, or speaking up in a meeting, you might encounter these sabotaging thoughts. Train your mind to handle them by practising meditation, mindfulness, and postponing worry time. It's a simple yet powerful strategy that truly works!

2. Reframe Challenges as Strengths

Strength mapping helps transform challenges into opportunities to leverage your skills.

What is Strength Mapping?

- Take a piece of paper and write down your talents, gifts, knowledge, and skills.
- Identify your top five most prominent strengths.
- Reflect on tasks you dislike or areas where your strengths feel underutilised.

For example:

If you frequently perform repetitive tasks that feel draining, identify one of your strengths—such as creativity or analytical thinking, and find ways to apply it. This shift in perspective can make those tasks more engaging and meaningful.

3. Shift Your Approach

Once you've identified underutilised strengths, brainstorm ways to integrate them into your current role or daily life. For example:

- Use creativity to introduce innovation in a structured environment.
- Leverage empathy to enhance team dynamics or improve communication.
- Apply problem-solving skills to tackle recurring issues in a more effective way.
  By actively using your strengths, you'll find greater satisfaction and purpose in your work and personal endeavours.

Renowned coach Brewerton Brooks emphasised that focusing on your strengths leads to improvements in **PACE**, which stands for **Performance, Agility, Confidence, and Energy**. Here's how each aspect is positively influenced:

- **Performance**: Leveraging your strengths allows you to perform tasks more efficiently and effectively. When you work within your natural abilities, you produce better results with less effort, leading to greater productivity and success.

Reflecting on my own experience, I vividly recall the advice from one of my line managers during a period when I was struggling with negative self-talk: "Always look at the wonderful

things you've done. Do more of it." Those words shifted my perspective and helped me refocus on what I could do in situations where things weren't going as expected.

This advice gave me the courage to concentrate on my strengths, regain belief in myself, and approach my role with renewed confidence. By focusing on what I was good at, I was able to improve my performance and make consistent progress every day. It highlights the transformative power of leveraging your strengths to overcome challenges and achieve success.

- **Agility**: A strengths-focused approach enhances your ability to adapt to changing circumstances. Instead of being bogged down by weaknesses, you can apply your strengths creatively to navigate challenges and seize opportunities, making you more resilient in dynamic environments.

When I first moved to the UK after a successful 18-year career journey, it felt like starting all over again. I came as a student, balancing part-time work while caring for my family alongside my husband. It was both a mental and physical struggle, as the path ahead was uncertain. I found myself in a VUCA (volatile, uncertain, complex, and ambiguous) world, doubting my skills and comparing myself to others in this completely new environment.

However, my past experiences had equipped me with resilience and the belief that I could overcome challenges. Instead of being bogged down by my weaknesses, I focused on my strengths and fought for the right opportunity. This persistence led me to become a Lecturer in the UK, embarking on a brand-new career journey. Life, in its mysterious ways, connected the dots for me, aligning my passion for teaching and training with my professional goals.

As a job seeker, no matter your age or background, you are bound to face challenges. The key is to embrace a growth mindset, believe in yourself, and trust in your strengths. With determination and self-belief, the right opportunities will find their way to you.

- **Confidence**: Recognising and using your strengths fosters a sense of self-assurance. When you are aware of your unique capabilities and apply them, you develop trust in your ability to handle situations, which naturally boosts your confidence.

I believe confidence is a precious jewel we should wear every day. When you carry it, others can see it reflected in your personality. Think about how animals fall prey to predators; the moment they sense fear, the predator takes control. Similarly, in life, if you exude confidence and believe in yourself, you often find the world responding to your energy. The world around you are constantly testing your resolve, waiting for you to falter.

Opportunities are naturally drawn to those who display confidence. It starts with your thoughts, what you think, you believe, and what you believe shapes your actions. Every time you walk into a room, wear that confidence-like armour. It will not only multiply positive "sage" feelings but also position you to seize the opportunities that await. When you walk out of that room, you'll carry with you the satisfaction of having given your best. Confidence isn't just a mindset, it's a magnet for success.

- **Energy**: Working within your strengths is energising. Tasks aligned with your strengths feel less like work and more like purpose-driven action, reducing burnout and increasing your enthusiasm for what you do.

When talking about energy, I'm reminded of an insightful book I read called Power of *Human Energy* by Kala Flynn. In it, she discusses three key states of energy:

1. **Power Down** – This is the phase where we stop, ground ourselves, rest, and breathe in order to recharge and regain energy.
2. **Power Up** – Here, we activate ourselves through mental motivation, praise, or inspiration, building momentum and focus for our actions.
3. **Power Through** – This is the state where we convert our physical, mental, and emotional energy into action, allowing us to achieve daily goals and tackle challenges.

In our constant battle through life, it is important to power down and re charge in your own way listening to your body. This will help you to power up and power through in a way that you even could not imagine.

By focusing on our strengths, we minimise energy waste, enabling us to stay in the Power Through state for longer periods. This is why some people seem to possess boundless energy as they pursue life. They've mastered the art of aligning their actions with their strengths, making their energy flow more efficiently.

By embracing this strengths-based approach, you not only enhance your ability to excel but also cultivate a fulfilling and sustainable rhythm in both your professional and personal life. As Brooks highlights, **PACE** isn't just about moving forward; it's about moving forward with purpose and alignment. By building on your strengths, you're likely to be more engaged and fulfilled in your work.

Applying Strengths in Your Career

When looking for a job, take the time to examine the job description and identify the core responsibilities. Then, think about which of your strengths align with those responsibilities.

If the job requires strong interpersonal skills, for example, and you're naturally empathetic, highlight that strength in your application. The more your strengths align with the role, the happier, more productive, and more energetic you'll feel at work.

Avoiding "Strength Overdrive"

While leveraging your strengths is crucial, over-relying on one can lead to imbalance. For example, an accountant with strong attention to detail may focus so much on minor elements that they miss the big picture or micromanage others. Balance and flexibility are key; use your strengths wisely but remain open to growth in other areas.

By recognising and building on your strengths, you'll enter the job market with confidence and clarity. You'll know what makes you valuable, and you'll be ready to contribute in ways that feel natural and fulfilling. Embrace this strength-based approach as you launch your career, it will set you on a path toward success and personal growth.

Your Habits

"We first make our Habits, then our habits make us."

-John Dryden-

A wise man once said, *"You can identify a successful person simply by looking at their daily routine."*

Take a moment to reflect—what does success mean to you? More importantly, what daily habits do you need to cultivate to support that vision? Your routines shape your progress, so aligning them with your goals is key to achieving lasting success.

We all want to build good habits! But we often fail. Let's explore more.

Building Habits Matters

In *Atomic Habits*, James Clear describes habits as *"behaviours that become automatic through repetition"*. Habits make life easier by allowing us to handle routine tasks with minimal energy and effort. However, many of us start new activities, learning an instrument, working out, reading regularly, only to give up before they become habits. This happens because we haven't repeated these actions enough for them to stick. Research suggests that it takes about 21 days of repetition for an action to start becoming a habit. So, if you're struggling to reach your goals or feel stuck, it's time to look at your existing habits and see how they align with the future you want to create.

As a job seeker, you're working towards a big goal: landing a role that aligns with your career aspirations. Think about that goal and envision the kind of person you want to be once you achieve it. Now, look at your current self, what small wins or changes will help you bridge that gap?

Building positive habits now can help you move toward your goals step by step. Each small habit you establish brings you closer to the person you want to become and helps you stand out in a competitive job market.

Habit Stacking: An Easy Way to Build New Habits

James Clear introduces the concept of "habit stacking," where you link a new habit with an existing one to make it easier to adopt. Let's try an activity to help you get started:
1. **List Your Daily Actions**: Write down everything you do in a typical day.
2. **Label Each Action**: For each action, note if it's a natural habit (something you do automatically), a positive habit, or an ineffective habit. (I do not like to call Bad or good habits)

Ex.

	Effective Habit	Natural	In effective Habit
Wake up		X	
Switch off the Alarm		X	
Check the phone			X
Go bathroom		X	
Weigh my self	X		
10 mins Yoga	X		
Brush my teeth	X		
Have a shower	X		
Hang up towel to Dry	X		
Get Dressed		X	
List continue			

3. **Stack New Habits**: Identify effective and/ or Natural habits / routines and find ways to incorporate new habits alongside them.

For example:
- **After I wake up** [Natural Habit] **I'll drink a glass of water** [New Habit].
- **After 10 minutes of stretching** [Existing Habit], **I'll review my tasks for the day** [New Habit].
- **After I get dressed** [Natural Habit], **I'll check job postings online** [New Habit].

Building these small habits, like regularly checking job postings, can have a significant impact over time as they add up to help you reach your career goals.

Implementation Intention : Setting Habits

As per James Clear, one powerful technique to reinforce habits is to use an "implementation intention." This involves **stating when and where** you'll carry out a habit in a specific way, like this:
- **"When I wake up in the morning, I'll meditate for 5 minutes in bed."**
- **"I will [action] at [time] in [location]."**

This approach gives your habit a clear time and place, making it easier to remember and follow through.

Create mini habits that take no more than two minutes to implement. The most important step is simply *starting* your desired habit. Think of it like entering a highway—once you're on, the rest will follow naturally.

For example, if you want to make yoga your first activity after waking up, set a habit intention like: *"When I wake up, I will change into my workout outfit."* This small action makes it easier to follow through with the full habit.

Environment and Social Influence on Habits

The culture and environment you're in heavily influence which habits feel natural. We're more likely to adopt behaviours that are praised by those around us, especially by close friends, family, or people we admire. Steve Judge, in his book **"GOLD"**, refers to finding a supportive community as building your **"golden gang",** a group of people who encourage your positive habits and hold you accountable. (You will explore more in Chapter 4).

To develop positive habits, surround yourself with people who share similar goals or values. This can help reinforce your new habits and make them easier to maintain. For example, if you want to improve your professional skills, consider joining a group or community of people who share that focus as an example; Join a Toastmasters Club to develop public speaking skills.

I discovered the need to develop my communication skills during a presentation at work during the early stage of my career. My mentor advised me to join a Toastmasters club, and that decision turned out to be one of the best blessings in my life. The people I met there provided invaluable feedback that helped me improve my skills. Later, I took on a leadership role, forming a new club and becoming its charter president of the "Kaduwela Toastmasters Club" in Sri Lanka. Through that experience, I not only developed my abilities but also built a valuable network of contacts who have supported me in thriving, even beyond my home country.

This experience reinforced my belief in the power of community—but it's essential to choose the right one. Surrounding yourself with the right people can elevate your growth and success.

Why This Matters for Your career

Creating habits might seem like a small step, but for an individual who preserves a job opportunity, they're invaluable. The job market is competitive, and standing out requires a strong sense of self. By clarifying your goals, then revisiting your daily routines to see how well they support those goals, you can identify gaps and make intentional improvements.

This bring down to creating your supportive network , looking at potential career opportunities daily, building habits around the skills required for your dream career etc.

When you build habits around small wins, you're consistently moving closer to your aspirations, making steady progress instead of waiting for sudden changes. By integrating these habits into your daily life, you'll grow into the professional you want to become.

Remember: "**If you keep doing what you did yesterday, you'll stay the same**." Embrace small, positive changes today to create a better future.

What I Want to Become

Imagine you are at a bus stop, unsure of where to go. Without a destination in mind, you cannot decide which bus to board. Life works the same way. Each day, we make choices that shape our path. But without clarity about what we want, those choices can lack direction.

Our brains are equipped with a **Reticular Activating System (RAS)**, a powerful filter that processes millions of stimuli and helps us make decisions, both consciously and unconsciously. When we set clear goals, our subconscious mind aligns itself to recognise opportunities and make decisions that bring us closer to those goals. Most of the time, we operate on autopilot, guided by patterns and commands stored in our subconscious. Professor Steve Peters explains this well in his book "*The Mind Management*". That's why it's essential to train our minds and consciously set life goals.

Self-Luminosity

To decide your direction, you first need to understand yourself:
- **Who are you?**
- **What motivates you?**
- **What do you want?**

We often wait for someone else to ignite the light within us, a mentor, a friend, or a life-changing event. But the truth is, a lamp cannot be illuminated by someone else. Others can provide a spark or inspire us, but the real illumination comes from within, fuelled by our own energy and purpose.

This is the essence of self-luminosity. It's the ability to shine brightly from within, powered by self-awareness and self-motivation. Self-luminosity, in other words, called "Self-awareness", is the "fuel" that keeps your inner light burning. It helps you understand:

- Your strengths and weaknesses.
- Your passions and fears.
- Your goals and what drives you.

Rather than waiting for external validation, take time to reflect on who you are. Use some of the time you spend on social media, scrolling through others' lives, to focus inward. Ask yourself:

- What do I truly want in life?
- What makes me unique?
- How can I grow and contribute to the world?

Before trying to understand the world around you, invest time in understanding yourself. When you are clear about who you are and what you want, you no longer need to rely on others to light your way. You become your own source of strength, resilience, and inspiration.

Remember, self-luminosity isn't about seeking approval or waiting for external forces to guide you. It's about recognising that the power to shine lies within you. Once you embrace this, your light can illuminate not only your path but also inspire those around you.

Once you gain this clarity, setting goals becomes easier. For instance, many young people dream of starting a business. While the success rate of startups is only 1.5%, this rate improves significantly for those aged 30–40, often because they spend their earlier years gaining experience, skills, and capital by working in businesses. Jack Ma's advice provides a practical framework for different life stages, emphasizing the importance of learning, growth, and contribution.

Here's how this aligns with having a clear direction in life:

1. **20–30 years: Learn by working for someone**
   At this stage, gaining knowledge, skills, and experience is crucial. Working for someone provides exposure to different industries, mentors, and organisational practices, which form the foundation for future aspirations.
2. **30–40 years: Start your own business**
   With the experience and network gained in the previous decade, this is an ideal time to take calculated risks and turn your vision into reality. This phase aligns with leveraging the skills and confidence you have built.
3. **40–50 years: Grow your business**
   By this stage, you're better equipped to scale your business, mentor others, and make a lasting impact. The focus shifts to sustainability, expansion, and leading effectively.
4. **50+ years: Share your knowledge and enjoy life**
   Having achieved personal and professional milestones, this is a time to give back—mentoring others, sharing insights, and finding joy in personal and social contributions.

This roadmap helps align life choices with aspirations by breaking down goals into manageable phases. It encourages individuals to prioritize growth, seize opportunities at the right time, and contribute meaningfully, leading to a fulfilling life.

Reflect and Plan

During my final year of university, I secured my first job. However, at the time, I didn't know what career suited me. I simply decided to give my best to whatever opportunity came my way. Looking back, I realize that if I had spent a few moments reflecting and planning, I could have accelerated my journey toward success.

Take time now to ask yourself:

- What do I want?
- Where do I see myself in 5–10 years?
- What steps can I take today to move closer to my vision?

Instead of relying solely on others' opinions or societal norms, focus on what truly matters to you. Avoid shortcuts; life doesn't offer quick fixes for success. True success comes from smart work, consistent effort, and the right choices.

Visualising Your Future

Close your eyes and picture yourself in the year in next 5 years. Imagine the best version of your life:

Example:

- You've completed your degree.
- You've started a job you love.
- You've bought your first car, think about your favourite brand
- You're confident, happy, and fulfilled.

Now, open your eyes and think: What steps do you need to take today to make that vision a reality? Break your goals into smaller, achievable milestones. Personal Development guru, Brain Tracy explained in his Goal setting session that it is important to make those affirmations in "Present Tense". It will signal your brain as if you achieve them.

For example:

Step-by-Step Plan	When	Actions Now
Complete the degree with distinction	2026	Join a supportive study group and focus.
Join ABC Company as IT Administrator	2027	Build connections with people at the company and industry.
Complete Microsoft Cloud Certification	2027	Study prerequisites and enrol in the program.
Buy a red Suzuki Swift	2028	Save a fixed amount monthly; explore investments.
Earn a second certification	2029	Research prerequisites and start planning.
Work as a Cloud Computing Engineer at Microsoft	2030	Develop skills (e.g., communication, programming, IELTS).

By breaking goals into manageable steps, you'll feel more confident and motivated. Each step you complete will bring you closer to your ultimate vision.

The Power of Visualisation

Visualisation is a powerful tool for success. Everything we create first exists in our minds as a thought. Yet, we often dwell on negative emotions, fear, anger, or doubt, instead of focusing on what we want.

Here's how you can use visualisation:
1. **Draw Your Dreams:** Sketch your goals, like the life you want to lead or the things you want to achieve.
2. **Create a Vision Board:** Collect images of your dream car, home, career, or lifestyle. Use them as your phone or computer wallpaper.
3. **Immerse Yourself:** Carry reminders of your goals, photos, affirmations, or symbols of success.

I met a talented young gentleman during the Trainer Certification Program conducted by DAASH Global. What inspired me most was his unique way of focusing on his dreams.Every morning, he would take a dollar bill from his wallet, smell it, and visualize his future earnings in dollars. He even had a presentation on his screen displaying his dreams and goals. His dedication was unwavering.

Within a year, Tony moved to Dubai, joined a real estate company, and started building his career. I later saw him on social media, giving interviews and passionately sharing his journey. His consistency, commitment, and dedication were truly remarkable—I knew he was destined for success. Eventually, he launched his own lucrative real estate company in Dubai, turning his vision into reality.

I've also witnessed **Steve Judge**, a renowned motivational speaker, share how visualization transformed his life. By drawing his dreams, he eventually became a World Champion. As a student, I attended one of his talks at Nottingham Trent University, and his message truly resonated with me. Inspired, I decided to apply it to my own life. I drew a picture of myself as a *Lecturer at a University in the UK* and pasted it inside my diary. I also turned on job notifications for lecturer positions and continuously visualized this goal.

One day, I came across the perfect job opportunity, so I sent my application. A week later, I got my first interview—and it turned out to be the final one. That's how I became a *Course Director and Lecturer at MK:U – Cranfield University*.Since then, I have used this technique to turn other dreams into reality, from designing my first conference and buying my dream vehicle to now publishing this book.
No doubt, visualization can work for you as well!

Visualising your dreams is essential to staying focused and motivated on your journey toward success. **A vision board** as a screensaver is a powerful way to keep your goals visible daily, constantly reminding you of what you aim to achieve. Similarly, maintaining a **goal journal** or dream diary allows you to document your aspirations with photos, quotes, and reflections, making your dreams tangible and emotionally engaging. Placing sticky notes or **goal cards** in frequently visible places can reinforce your commitment, while affirmations and mind maps can clarify and organise your goals, engaging both your conscious and subconscious mind. The key is to combine these Visualisation techniques with actionable steps, regularly reviewing your progress and celebrating milestones to stay on track.

Personally, I would use a digital vision board for daily reminders, complemented by a goal journal to document and reflect on my progress. By choosing a method that resonates with you, you can ensure that your dreams remain at the forefront of your mind, inspiring purposeful action every day. This practice ties into the **Law of Attraction** and **Law of Vibration**, your thoughts and emotions create energy that aligns with your goals.

Keep Your Goals Close

While it's tempting to share your goals with others, be cautious. Talking too much about your plans can dilute their excitement and expose you to doubts or negativity. Instead, cherish your goals privately and let your achievements speak for themselves. Seek guidance only from trusted mentors or friends who genuinely support you (Chapter 04). Remember, no one knows your potential better than you do.

What does success mean to you ?

Success is unique for everyone. Take time to define it for yourself:
- Is it financial independence?
- Landing your dream job?
- Exploring the world?
- Building a happy family?
- Staying healthy and vibrant?

Once you define success, set specific goals that align with your vision. You know where you want to go. Now reflect on where you are and who you are and stat creating that step-by-step journey ahead.

The journey to success begins with **clarity, planning, and visualization**. Write down your goals, break them into actionable steps, and keep your vision alive in your mind. Build positive habits into your daily routine that drive your success.
Focus on your strengths and stay true to your values. Maintain the right mindset and attitude to push through challenges. By doing so, you'll unlock your potential and achieve what once seemed impossible.

Are you ready to take ownership of your life and design your future?

Start today, the possibilities are endless.

In summary

- Knowing yourself is the foundation for a fulfilling and successful career.
- Understanding your true personality can guide you in selecting a career that aligns with your strengths and values.
- By developing the right mindset and focusing on your goals while developing useful habits to drive step by step is crucial to achieve success as an early career professional.
- When you work in an environment that fits your core traits, you're more likely to be engaged and perform well.
- Based on all these findings and reflections you had so far, now formulate your own SWOT analysis. This will summarize your internal strengths and weaknesses, as well as the external threats and opportunities that can help you effectively plan your career.

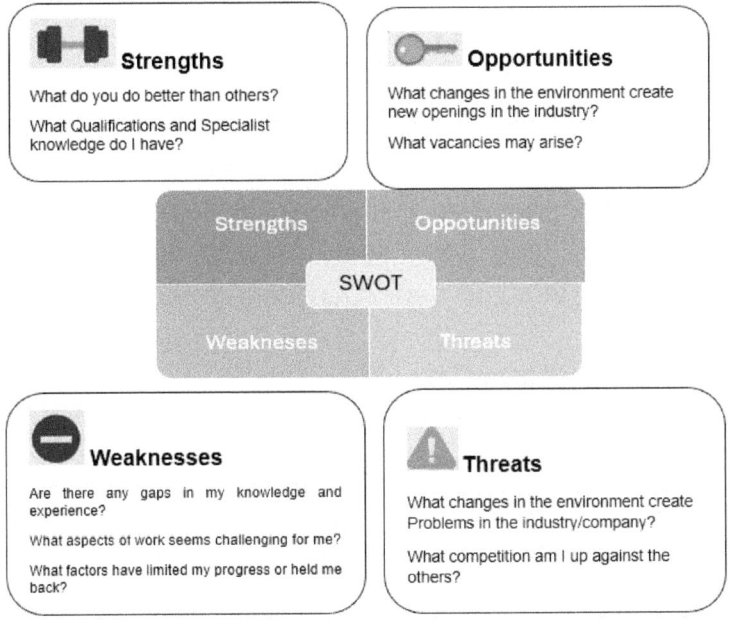

- *Figure 8 - Personal SWOT*

03

Taking Charge of Your Future

"Accept responsibility for your life. Know that You who will get you where you want to be. No one else."

– Les Brown

As a seedling determined to grow and thrive, knowing where you want to go and how far you need to reach is essential for planning your journey. Just as a seedling stretches toward the sunlight, a individual must have clarity about their destination and the steps required to get there. With a clear vision and purposeful effort, you can transform into something greater, reaching the heights you aspire to achieve. now.

After reading this Chapter, you will be able to:

- Identify whether you are career ready
- Articulate Transferable skills from your experience and extra-curricular activities
- Analyse your Skills GAP and develop an action plan

Are you Career Ready?

Career Planning is the process of understanding your strengths, skills, and aspirations to identify and pursue a fulfilling and successful career path. It involves setting career goals, creating a roadmap, and making intentional decisions that align with your interests, values, and abilities. This process is not static. It evolves with your experiences, new opportunities, and the changing dynamics of the world of work.

Most often when companies analyse the career readiness of individuals in different ways. Look at some of the questions they use to check individual career readiness and rate where you are from 1 -10.(1 being weak and 10 being excel.)

Career Readiness area	Your rating
Being able to communicate well with people from different backgrounds	
Being able to work in a step-by-step way to get the job done in time	
Being able to use your own initiative to solve problems	
Being able to get on with people in a caring, supportive way	
Being able to focus on task and be assertive when required	
Being able to work quickly and efficiently to meet deadline	

When you plan your career, you set a direction. While this path won't always be linear, planning helps you remain focused and adaptable when faced with crossroads. By actively reviewing and adjusting your career plan, you ensure that it remains relevant and aligned with your evolving ambitions. What's most crucial is to take ownership of your journey,moving consciously through it and making informed decisions.

Why Career Planning Matters?

Where you want to go!

Where you are now!

The diagram illustrates your opportunities represented as dots of various sizes. You have multiple paths to reach your destination, and the outcome depends on which opportunities you choose to pursue and the path you take. Often, we find ourselves confused by the abundance of options and lose our way.

Reflecting on my own career journey as **early career professionals,** I often wish I had received more career advice during my school and university years. Like many, I navigated my career by connecting random dots, drawing inspiration from experiences and opportunities without a structured plan. While this approach offered lessons, I now realize that proactive planning could have led to greater satisfaction and achievement.

This is why planning and seeking guidance from a mentor can be invaluable, helping you save time and energy. A mentor can be someone from your family, friends, colleagues, or a professional outside your immediate circle. They can provide fresh perspectives and decode complex information based on their experience.

Richard Bolles, in his book; *What Color Is Your Parachute?* emphasises the importance of understanding yourself deeply to find roles that truly align with your strengths and aspirations. Too often, we rely on the "Spray and Pray" technique, sending out countless CVs across networks and passively waiting for opportunities to come our way. However, true success lies in focusing on what you need, aligning your actions with your goals, and seeking workplaces where you can thrive. Having reflected deeply on my own experiences, my mission is to provide the guidance I once needed, empowering you to approach your career with clarity, intention, and purpose. By understanding yourself and taking targeted steps, you can discover fulfilling opportunities that resonate with who you are.

Finding the Best Career Fit

This is one of the most common questions young individuals ask me during one-on-one or group mentoring sessions. It's important to remember that there is no single job role set in stone for anyone; you are constantly evolving along with the world around you. The key is to identify potential opportunities and decide which ones to pursue.

Career-Defining Triangle

Now, apply the findings of Chapter 2 about your inner self to identify the best career fit. This explains how you can align your personality, position, and individual self (persona) with an identified job opportunity. Always consider these three career-defining elements as a triangle. Professor Ajantha Dharmasiri is explained the importance of this alignment in his talks. I truly believe this model accurately reflects my own experience and provides a solid framework for career development.

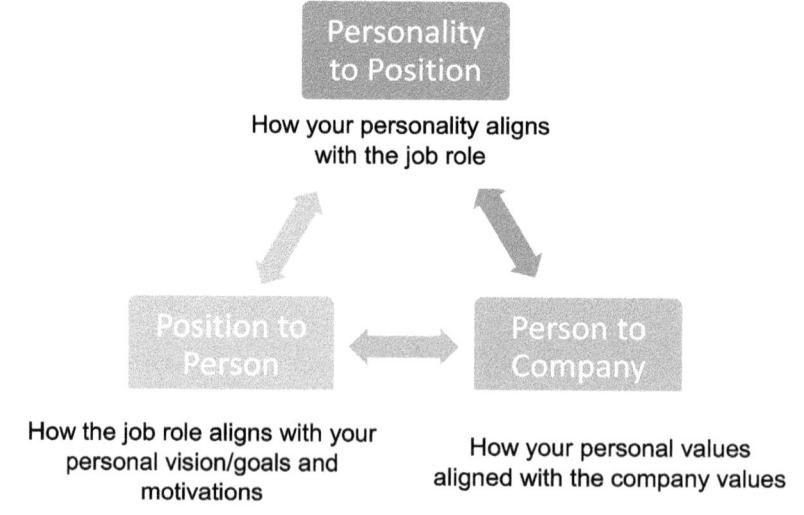

Figure 9 - Career Defining Triangle

If you are **early career professionals** and have not yet figured what is best for you. Try answering these questions by yourself.

1. What options does your educational pathway offer?

If you are currently studying or have completed a degree or vocational training, it indicates a level of interest or skill in that field. This provides a foundation to explore related opportunities. For instance, if you're studying business management, you have a wide range of career options, while technical students often have predefined roles aligned with their field of study.

List down potential roles in your field. Identify one that excites you, offers the lifestyle you desire, and meets your financial goals.

2. What inspires you?

Often, people look up to family members, friends, or community figures who are considered "successful role models." While these role models can provide inspiration, it's important to reflect on whether their career aligns with your strengths, personality, and passions. Ask yourself:

- Is this something you truly love doing?
- Does it allow you to use your strengths to their fullest?

3. Reflect on feedback from others.

Seek feedback from your "cheerleaders" those who know you well and can highlight your strengths and talents (Refer the sheet that you filled in Chapter 2). This can help you understand how others perceive you and what you excel at.

Use this insight to identify potential job roles. Research their job descriptions to assess if they match your skills and interests.

4. Use online tools for additional guidance.

Take advantage of psychometric tests and career exploration platforms to get tailored suggestions. Some excellent resources include:
- **Psychometric Tests**
- **CareerExplorer.com**
- **Skills Matcher (by O*NET)**
- **LinkedIn Career Explorer**
- **123test Career Aptitude Test**
- **Princeton Review Career Quiz**
- **MAPP Career Test**

These tools can provide evaluations and potential job matches based on your interests, strengths, and skills.

Understanding Job Descriptions

Companies provide job descriptions to outline the responsibilities, expectations, and skills required for specific roles. These descriptions serve as valuable tools for understanding industry demands and planning your career path. A great starting point for analysing job requirements is *ONET Online (www.onetonline.org), where you can search for job titles and review detailed descriptions to gain insights into the responsibilities and skills needed. In addition to ONET, job* descriptions can be found on platforms like LinkedIn, indeed, company career websites, newspapers, and recruitment agency sites. These resources collectively help you identify the skills to develop, tailor your applications, and align your career goals with market opportunities.

The Job Analysis Table

Based on your initial search for potential jobs, you can create a job analysis table to streamline your decision-making process and prioritize your job search effectively. This table allows you to compare roles systematically, helping you identify common trends and align your goals. By analysing multiple job descriptions, you can uncover:

- **Common Expectations**: Understanding the key qualifications, responsibilities, and traits employers consistently seek for your target role.
- **Skill Gaps**: Identifying areas where your expertise or experience may need enhancement to meet market demands.
- **Salary Benchmarks**: Gaining a realistic perspective on compensation, enabling you to set informed expectations and negotiate confidently.

Creating a job analysis table empowers you to approach your career search with clarity, targeting roles where you can thrive while addressing any gaps to increase your competitiveness.

Company & Job Role	Key Responsibilities	Skills Required	Salary Range
[Example Company]	[Responsibilities from job description]	[Skills listed in job post]	[Salary details if given]

Here is an example for different entry-level jobs.

Company & Job Role	Key Responsibilities	Skills Required	Salary Range
ABC Corp - Marketing Assistant	Assist with campaign planning, manage social media accounts, conduct market research, and coordinate with teams to	Communication, organisational skills, proficiency in marketing tools (e.g., Google Analytics, Canva).	£20,000 - £25,000/year (UK)

	execute marketing strategies.		
XYZ Ltd - Data Analyst Intern	Analyse datasets to identify trends, prepare reports, assist in implementing data solutions, and ensure data accuracy and consistency.	SQL, Excel, statistical tools (e.g., R or Python), attention to detail, problem-solving skills.	$30,000 - $40,000/year (US)
Tec Solutions - IT Support Analyst	Provide technical support, troubleshoot hardware/software issues, assist in system upgrades, and maintain technical documentation.	Customer service, troubleshooting, basic network and system knowledge, familiarity with IT systems.	€25,000 - €30,000/year (EU)
Retail Works - Store Associate	Manage inventory, assist customers, handle transactions, and maintain store cleanliness and visual merchandising standards.	Interpersonal skills, customer service, time management, ability to handle POS systems.	£18,000 - £22,000/year (UK)

Figure 10 - Sample Job Analysis Table

RRS Matrix

Identify a job posting that interests you and list down its main responsibilities and required skills in the **RRS Matrix (Role - Responsibility -Skills) Table** below. For each skill, rate your current proficiency on a scale of 1 to 10 (1 being very low and 10 being outstanding). Based on this, identify the skills that rated 5 or below first. Then take actions to develop to successfully perform each responsibility. This process will give you a clear list of areas to focus on for your professional growth.

Sample - RRS matrix

Role: *Marketing Assistant* role:

Responsibility	Required Skills	Your Rating (1-10)	Skills to Develop
Assist with campaign planning	Communication, creativity, project management	8 5 4	Enhance creativity through brainstorming techniques and learn project management tools (e.g., Trello).
Manage social media accounts	Digital Marketing, Negotiation Communication	5 6 8	Explore advanced social media analytics tools (e.g., Hootsuite).
Conduct market research	Analytical skills, Excel proficiency, Data Analysis & Interpretation	4 8 5	Improve proficiency in Data analysis and complete a Google Analytics certification.
Coordinate with teams to execute strategies	Teamwork, Organisational skills, time management	7 5 5	Develop advanced time management techniques and improve task prioritization.

Figure 11 - Example of RRS matrix

This is another way you can visually create this, Matrix.

Job Role: Marketing Assistant   -Skills Audit

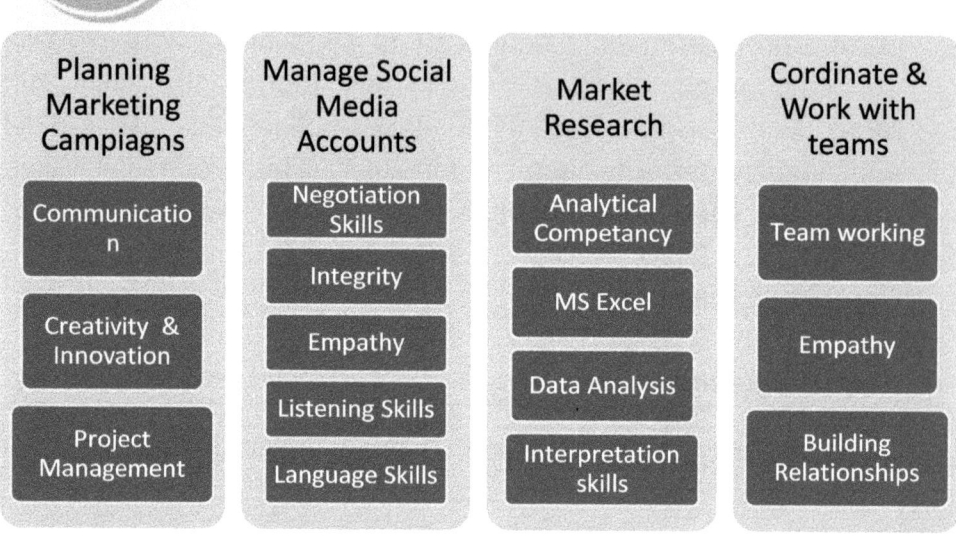

Planning Marketing Campiagns	Manage Social Media Accounts	Market Research	Cordinate & Work with teams
Communication	Negotiation Skills	Analytical Competancy	Team working
	Integrity	MS Excel	
Creativity & Innovation	Empathy		Empathy
	Listening Skills	Data Analysis	
Project Management	Language Skills	Interpretation skills	Building Relationships

This method helps you prioritize skill development for the role you aspire to and sets a clear roadmap for your career advancement. Now prepare this list as given below, which will give you a clear understanding of your skills. This reflection provides a clear picture of Your current capabilities, skills you need to develop to meet industry expectations, Actionable areas for improvement.

Areas that **I am good at;** Skills rated from 6-10 -	Areas that **I need to work on;** Skills rated from 1-5

Action Plan: From Gaps to Growth

Once you've mapped your target role:

1. Prioritize Skill Development: Focus on critical areas like communication, technical tools, or customer service practices.
2. Seek Learning Opportunities: Attend workshops, online courses, or certifications tailored to your skill gaps.
3. Gain Practical Experience: Look for internships, part-time roles, or volunteering opportunities that align with your target responsibilities.

An Upward Spiral

Career planning is not a linear path. It's an **upward spiral** of growth and self-discovery. Each step in your career builds upon the last, with opportunities to refine your goals and actions.

Here's how this iterative process works:

- **Regularly Evaluate Your Progress**:
  Periodically assess where you stand compared to your goals. Reflect on your achievements, identify areas for improvement, and ensure your actions align with your evolving aspirations.

- **Adapt Your Goals Based on New Opportunities and Insights**:
  As you gain experience and encounter new opportunities, your perspective and priorities may shift. Be open to adjusting your career goals to align with these changes while staying true to your core values and long-term vision.

- **Continuously Learn and Grow**:
  Embrace learning as a lifelong journey. Develop new skills, seek feedback, and take on challenges that push you out of your comfort zone. Growth is a dynamic process that propels your career forward.

By adopting this mindset, you transform career planning into a proactive, empowering process. Each iteration brings you closer to fulfilling your potential, equipping you with the confidence and clarity to navigate your professional journey with purpose.

Skills Signalling

The recent LinkedIn survey report titled *"Skills Gap or Signalling Gap?"* sheds light on critical challenges in youth employment, especially in emerging markets such as Brazil, India, Indonesia, and South Africa. Employers in these regions are actively seeking entry-level talent with a blend of diverse technical, soft, and computer literacy skills. There is a growing demand for advanced ICT and Fourth Industrial Revolution (4IR) skills. While youth profiles tend to reflect a solid grasp of technical skills, there is a noticeable underrepresentation of soft skills, such as communication and teamwork, which employers highly value. This discrepancy points to a significant "skills signalling gap". Young individuals possess the skills but often fail to showcase or prioritize them.

This gap underscores the importance of not only developing the right skills but also effectively signalling them to potential employers. It is essential for young people to recognise the full value of their soft skills, which play a crucial role in long-term career success. The report also emphasises the need for greater investment in youth employment programs, career counselling, and campaigns that encourage increased usage of digital platforms. Aligning training with market demands and improving the accessibility of labour market data are also key strategies to address this issue.

In the context of the rapidly evolving jobs landscape in today's VUCA (Volatility, Uncertainty, Complexity, and Ambiguity) world, continuous self-evaluation of skills is crucial. It's important to identify any gaps and take proactive steps to bridge them to stay relevant in an ever-changing market.

I -T & X Shape Skills

This insight is a reminder that while technical expertise is undeniably important, equally crucial is the ability to communicate, collaborate, and adapt, skills that are often overlooked but are key to thriving in a dynamic and competitive work environment.

When identifying and categorising the professionals with different skills there are three different types.

I-shaped Skills: These individuals have deep expertise in a single area but lack the broader skill set to collaborate across different disciplines. While they are highly specialized, their narrow focus can limit their ability to work in cross-functional teams or adapt to new challenges.

T-shaped Skills: These professionals have deep knowledge and expertise in one area (represented by the vertical line of the 'T') and broad skills in various other areas, allowing them to collaborate effectively across disciplines (represented by the horizontal line). This balance makes them adaptable and valuable in diverse team settings.

X-shaped Skills: A more recent concept, X-shaped professionals combine the depth and breadth of T-shaped skills with additional strengths in leadership, empathy, and the ability to connect and manage teams. They are often seen as leaders who can inspire and coordinate efforts across different areas.

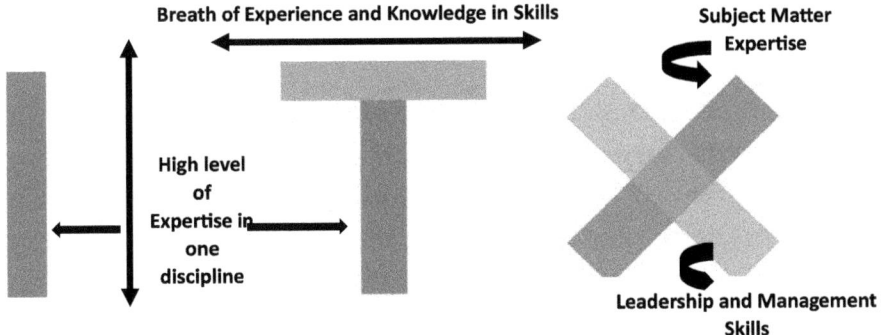

T-shaped employees are particularly sought after because they bring a versatile skill set that enables innovation, effective collaboration, and adaptability in rapidly changing environments. This framework, popularized by thought leaders like David Guest and Tim Brown, helps employers identify candidates who can contribute both as specialists and as integrative team players.

T-shaped skills are qualities and traits that certain professionals possess that make them valuable to an organization. Individuals with these skills typically have extensive knowledge and expertise in specific areas related to their professional performance and success as well as can easily train them to be X shape professionals.

What is the type of skills set you have.?

How you showcase your T Shape Skills in your CV?

To showcase your T-shaped skills in your CV, begin by identifying and highlighting your core expertise, such as technical skills, certifications, and experiences that demonstrate deep knowledge in your field. Complement this by emphasizing broad skills that reflect your cross-disciplinary capabilities, including collaboration, adaptability, and effective communication.

Tailor these skills to align with the job description, ensuring you include relevant keywords and examples. In the skills section, present a balanced list that combines both technical expertise and general competencies. Use action-oriented statements in your experience section to demonstrate how you've applied these skills in practical settings. Additionally, showcase your commitment to continuous learning by listing professional development efforts.

Example of T-Shaped Skills Section for a Computer Programmer CV:

Skills:

- Technical Expertise: Proficiency in C++, Python, JavaScript; in-depth understanding of algorithms and data structures; advanced knowledge of Linux and Windows operating systems; experience with database management (SQL, NoSQL)

- Broad Skills: Strong analytical and problem-solving abilities; effective communication and teamwork; project management; end-user orientation; adaptability to new technologies; networking and relationship building

By articulating both your specialized knowledge and broad skills, you effectively demonstrate your T-shaped abilities, making you an appealing candidate for roles that value versatility and depth.

Transferable Skills

As an early-career individual, you may not have extensive professional experience. However, the value you bring to potential employers lies in the **transferable skills** you've developed through your school education, extracurricular activities, certifications, and volunteer work.

What are Transferable Skills?
Transferable skills are abilities and qualities you've gained in one context (like school or extracurriculars) that can be applied effectively in another, such as the workplace. These include skills like problem-solving, teamwork, communication, time management, and leadership.

Reflecting on Your Experiences
Consider the activities you've engaged in and reflect on the skills you demonstrated. By analysing these experiences, you can draw connections between your current abilities and the requirements of the job you're targeting. Let's explore an example:

Example: You are applying for "Food Safety Analyst" position
Activity: Scouting Experience at School
- **What You Did:** Participated in outdoor survival activities, where you devised solutions to unexpected challenges, such as finding shelter or ensuring food was prepared safely.
- **Skills Demonstrated:** Problem-solving, attention to detail, adaptability, and resourcefulness.
- **Relevance to Food Safety Analyst Role:** These skills align with the job's focus on addressing challenges in

food preservation, quality control, and optimizing food production methods.

Activity: Participating in Charity Work (e.g., Prince Trust Step Challenge)

- **What You Did:** Completed 10,000 steps daily for a month, raising £1,120 to support children in need.
- **Skills Demonstrated:** Commitment, work ethic, perseverance, and social responsibility.
- **Relevance to Food Safety Analyst Role:** Demonstrates reliability, a strong sense of responsibility, and the ability to dedicate yourself to achieving goals; qualities highly valued in any professional role.

Incorporating Transferable Skills into Your Application

When applying for a position, it's crucial to clearly highlight your transferable skills in your:

1. **CV:**
   - Include a **Skills Section** where you outline your most relevant transferable skills.
   - Describe these experiences in your achievements, using action verbs to emphasise your contributions.
2. **Cover Letter:**
   - Explain how specific skills gained from your extracurricular activities align with the job description.
   - Provide concrete examples to show your capability and enthusiasm for the role.

3. **Interview**:
   o Be ready to share stories about your extracurricular activities and the skills you developed.
   o Use the **STAR Method (Situation, Task, Action, Result)** to effectively communicate your experiences.

Use a table like this to document your transferable skills. Use the given skills table to get inspiration on some of the skills.

Activity	Transferable Skills Acquired	Relevance to Job
Scouting Experience	Problem-solving, adaptability	Solving food preservation and quality control issues
Prince Trust Step Challenge	Commitment, work ethic	Demonstrating responsibility and dedication
Managing a School Club	Leadership, teamwork	Coordinating cross-functional projects
Completing Online Food Safety Course	Knowledge of hygiene practices	Foundational understanding of food safety principles

Why This Matters?

When you're an **early career professional**, your ability to **clearly articulate your transferable skills** sets you apart. Employers look for potential, not just experience. By reflecting on your extracurricular work and demonstrating its relevance, you present yourself as a capable and adaptable candidate. This approach will serve you well not only in crafting your CV and cover letter but also in making a strong impression during interviews. We'll dive deeper into these aspects in later chapters. You will explore further details of the above in Chapters 5 & 6.

In order to understand the skills and brainstorm skills, use can use the table below.

Skill Category	Reflection Prompts to Brainstorm Skills	Skills to Consider
Communication	Do you enjoy sharing ideas or giving presentations? Are you able to explain things clearly to others?	Verbal Communication, Written Communication, Public Speaking, Active Listening, Presentation Skills
Leadership	Have you led teams or projects? Are you comfortable making decisions and guiding others?	Team Management, Delegation, Motivational Skills, Conflict Resolution, Decision Making, Mentoring
Technical Expertise	Are you skilled with tools, software, or technologies? Have you solved technical problems or created new solutions?	Data Analysis, Programming (Python, Java), Excel, Database Management, Cloud Computing, Hardware Troubleshooting
Problem-Solving	Have you ever overcome a challenging situation? How did you approach it?	Critical Thinking, Analytical Thinking, Troubleshooting, Decision Making, Root Cause Analysis
Time Management	How do you handle deadlines? Can you organise your tasks and stay focused under pressure?	Task Prioritization, Meeting Deadlines, Multitasking, Focus, Stress Management, Calendar Management
Creativity	Have you contributed fresh ideas in your past work or hobbies? How do you express your creativity?	Idea Generation, Innovation, Artistic Design, Product Development, Content Creation, Conceptual Thinking
Collaboration	Are you a good team player? Do you enjoy working with others to achieve common goals?	Teamwork, Cross-functional Collaboration, Peer Support, Conflict Mediation, Knowledge Sharing
Adaptability	Can you easily adapt to new environments or changes? How do you handle unexpected situations?	Flexibility, Learning Agility, Change Management, Resilience, Open-mindedness, Stress Management
Customer Service	Have you worked directly with clients or customers?	Client Relations, Customer Support, Conflict Resolution, Needs

	How did you meet their needs and resolve issues?	Assessment, Product Knowledge, Upselling
Emotional Intelligence	How well do you understand and manage your emotions? Can you read and respond to the emotions of others?	Self-awareness, Empathy, Self-regulation, Social Skills, Motivation, Conflict Resolution
Analytical Thinking	Do you enjoy analysing information, identifying patterns, and making data-driven decisions?	Data Interpretation, Statistical Analysis, Research, Forecasting, Logical Reasoning, Problem Structuring
Negotiation	Have you ever successfully negotiated terms or deals? How do you balance assertiveness and empathy?	Persuasion, Conflict Resolution, Bargaining, Consensus Building, Compromise, Active Listening
Project Management	Have you managed a project from start to finish? How do you organise, plan, and execute tasks?	Project Planning, Budgeting, Resource Management, Risk Management, Scheduling, Deliverables Tracking, Team Coordination
Personal Development	How do you motivate yourself to grow personally and professionally? Are you open to learning new skills?	Self-reflection, Goal Setting, Lifelong Learning, Accountability, Self-discipline, Resilience
Resilience	Have you faced setbacks and bounced back? What strategies helped you keep going?	Stress Management, Positive Thinking, Adaptability, Determination, Emotional Regulation, Problem-Solving
Networking	Are you good at connecting with people and building relationships? Do you maintain professional contacts?	Relationship Building, Social Networking, Professional Networking, Follow-up, Relationship Management, Influence

In Summary

1. Career planning is an evolving process where individuals align their strengths, skills, and aspirations with career goals.
2. It involves reflecting on personal abilities and setting a direction while remaining adaptable to changing opportunities.
3. Companies assess career readiness by evaluating communication skills, initiative, task focus, and the ability to work with diverse people.
4. Planning your career aligning with the "Career Defining Triangle" helps you stay focused and navigate crossroads, making informed decisions along the way.
5. Reflecting on past experiences can reveal how proactive career planning could lead to greater satisfaction and achievement.
6. Career guidance from mentors can help streamline the journey by providing fresh perspectives and insights.
7. Identifying a career fit involves evaluating educational pathways, personal inspirations, feedback from others, and career tools.
8. Understanding job descriptions is crucial for aligning skills with industry needs, with tools like O*NET aiding in job research.
9. A Job Analysis Table helps assess key responsibilities, required skills, and salary benchmarks for informed career decisions.
10. The career planning process is iterative, requiring continuous self-reflection, goal adjustments, and skill development to stay relevant.

04

Building Your Personal Brand

"Your Network is your Net worth"

– Porter Gale

Just like a seedling reaching for the sky, your growth upward depends on the strength and depth of your roots. To thrive, you must expand your network of roots—connecting with diverse individuals and opportunities that nourish your journey. These roots represent your cohesive support system, offering vital nutrients of knowledge, collaboration, and encouragement to propel you forward.

A well-established network not only strengthens your foundation but also provides resilience during challenging times. By nurturing these connections and staying authentic, you cultivate a personal brand that is unique, adaptable, and deeply rooted in trust and collaboration, ensuring your continued growth and success.

At the end of reading this Chapter, you will be able to.

- Understand why and how you can create your Identity.
- Identify the importance of building your network of people who can influence your career success.
- Develop your Power Circle and manage those relationships effectively.

If you are an early career professional, you might not have realised the importance of your personal brand yet. Having a digital presence across multiple channels is not exactly "Personal Branding", Which is something beyond that and creating a "Purposeful" and "Meaningful" profile that complements your journey. Even if you are a working professional, personal branding is something very useful to effectively navigate through your career.

When you develop your personal brand there are three key aspects to think about. They are "Your Story", "Your Identity" and "Your Power Circle". Let's explore how you can build it through these three areas. Those three areas need to be clearly aligned. I will explain why?

Your Story

Each of us is unique, shaped by our upbringing, experiences, and the people we've engaged with throughout our lives. These elements come together to create a personal story, your story, that defines who you are and leaves a lasting impression on others. Your story is more than just a collection of events; it forms the foundation of your personal brand.

I was raised in a beautiful village in Sri Lanka, where the values instilled by my parents and grandparents became the cornerstone of my life. My grandfather, a man of simplicity and truth, was my role model. His unwavering commitment to helping anyone who came to him without expecting anything in return and his ability to cherish life's meaningful moments deeply inspired me as a child. His values influenced me profoundly, and I strive to embody the same principles in my life.

My parents' hard work and dedication to creating a better future for my brother and me taught me the importance of perseverance and commitment. Their sacrifices pushed me to pursue my own journey with determination and purpose. As we discussed in Chapter 2, under the section on Attitude, our environment shapes how we think and behave. These behaviours define our actions, and our actions ultimately craft our stories.

When someone asks, "What is your story?" remember that everyone has a unique narrative that reflects who they truly are. Your story is more than just a recount of past events; it embodies how you see the world, the values you hold dear, and the impact you aim to create. Let your story serve as the foundation for building a meaningful and authentic personal brand.

Take a moment to think about the values embedded in your story. Do they align with your true self? Too often, we see people trying to imitate others, mimicking behaviours that don't reflect their core identity. This approach is not only exhausting but also unsustainable. Your past, no matter how challenging or painful, plays a crucial role in shaping the person you are today. What matters most is how you've grown and transformed through those experiences.

I once had a conversation with a renowned young motivational speaker who shared his journey of overcoming drug addiction and a tumultuous childhood. By developing resilience, he turned his life around and now inspires thousands of young people across the globe. He owns his story unapologetically, sharing his experiences of transformation and growth to connect with others on a deep level.

When you step into an interview or any significant opportunity, what story will you bring to the table? How authentic will it be? The first and most important step in building a strong personal brand is owning your authentic story with pride. Be proud of who you are, exactly as you are, and let your story reflect the values and experiences that make you unique. Authenticity is the cornerstone of a personal brand that resonates and inspires.

How to Identify Your Story

Start by taking a piece of paper and writing down your memories without stopping for five minutes. Afterwards, reflect on those memories and identify patterns. What did you truly enjoy? What did you really value? Repeat this exercise several times to uncover deeper insights.

Then, pick a few of those stories and share them with a friend. Observe how they engage with your story and what they highlight. This feedback can help you understand which stories resonate most.

Think about the core message you can convey through each story. For example, how you studied for exams despite hardships and achieved great results, or how you took care of your elderly grandparents. Perhaps it's a memory of hiking with friends and the unforgettable experiences shared.

Reflect on these moments and identify the stories that you can articulate most clearly. Write them down, and use them in conversations to share your personal journey. By doing this, you'll begin to spread your story authentically, allowing others to connect with your unique experiences.

Your Identity

You already have an Authentic story. Now, ask yourself this critical question:

"Do others see me the way I see myself?"

If the answer is no, it's time to work on your identity.

Your personal brand, "who you are", needs to be clear and authentic. Imagine yourself as a product on a supermarket shelf. Why would someone choose you over other similar options? The answer lies in how the unique qualities and features of that product align with the customer's needs and expectations. Same as ours.

When someone hires you for their organisation, they have to see your unique identity that suits their needs and requirements.

Here's how you can make your identity stand out:

1. Focus on Your Core Strengths

If you are good at speaking and have a story that others recognise, it's essential to build on that strength. Whether you enjoy public speaking, storytelling, or motivational speaking, find a community where you can grow and share your voice. Joining groups like "Toastmasters" can provide you with opportunities to practice, receive feedback, and empower yourself to become an even stronger communicator.

If you have multiple skills, think of them as parts of a cohesive story that's easy for others to understand. Career expert John Lees refers to this as "holding positive pigeons." This means grouping your strengths in a way that makes sense and highlights the positive aspects of your abilities. For instance, if you're skilled in design, organisation, and leadership, frame these as complementary traits that showcase your ability to create, manage, and inspire. By aligning your strengths in this way, you create a clear and compelling narrative that others can easily grasp.

2. Be Memorable

What makes you stand out? Reflect on the qualities people most admire in you. It could be your creativity, your ability to organise events, your work with children, or your knack for storytelling. Whatever it is, identify these traits and amplify them.

Being memorable is about showcasing what you're naturally good at and what others value in you. I remember a colleague of mine whose name is "Pradeep". He was an incredible person with a unique ability to master any topic. He was passionate about digging deep and uncovering insights, which made him excel in many areas. Whenever we discussed any subject, he had so much to share. He was unique, and he brought joy and laughter to everyone around him. Even after 10 years, I still remember him vividly. The most important thing in any human relationship is how you make others feel. That feeling will stay with them for a long time.

Research suggests that if you engage with an individual for **7 hours**, across **11 interactions**, and on **4 different platforms**, you become easily memorable. This concept is crucial in shaping how you position yourself within a social context and build an **authentic personal brand**.

By consistently showing up across multiple touchpoints— whether through **professional networks, social media, public speaking, or written content**—you reinforce your identity, create trust, and leave a lasting impression. A strong personal brand not only helps establish credibility but also opens new opportunities in both personal and professional spheres.

3. Create Your Personal "Soundbite"

Your soundbite is a concise, 15-word statement that captures your strengths. It's something others might use to describe you when you're not in the room. If what you believe your soundbite to be matches what others say about you, then you've successfully created a clear and unique identity.

For example: "A dependable problem solver with a knack for creative solutions", "A dynamic organiser who turns ideas into impactful events", "An educator who inspires and empowers future leaders."

Kym Hamer, a leading personal branding expert, once discussed the concept of "Uber Talks"—how to introduce yourself briefly in any situation. She emphasised the importance of having this introduction ready and adaptable to various contexts.

John Lees, in his book, stresses the need for these statements to be natural and authentic. These statements should be simple, relevant, and warm enough to connect with people. When building your personal brand, others connect with you not just based on what you say, but on how you make them feel. Make sure your soundbite resonates with authenticity and warmth.

4. Craft a Proud Statement (Elevator Pitch)

A Proud Statement, also known as your Elevator Pitch, is one of the most important tools you can have in your personal branding toolkit. It is a concise, 30-60 seconds introduction that highlights who you are, what you do, and what you are looking for. This brief yet impactful statement is not only helpful in interviews but is also a versatile tool that can be used in a variety of situations to help people quickly understand your value. The key is to keep it simple, authentic, and memorable.

For example, consider this statement:
"I'm a passionate educator specialising in professional skills training. I help young individuals build their career pathways and develop confidence in their abilities. I'm currently looking to collaborate with organisations that value empowering early-career professionals."

This pitch clearly states who the person is, what they do, and what they are looking for, all while showcasing their passion for the work. Another example could be:

"I am a committed and ambitious professional specialising in creative design. With proven expertise in tailoring impactful designs to target audiences, I currently work as a freelance designer, collaborating with marketing agencies to bring their messages to life effectively. I am seeking an opportunity to join a leading organisation in creative advertising, where I can contribute my skills while advancing my professional growth."

By focusing on these elements, you can ensure that your identity is clear, authentic, and aligned with how others perceive you. A strong personal brand not only makes you memorable but also opens doors to new opportunities.

Many people find themselves uncertain about what to say or how to talk about themselves when introduced to someone for the first time. After all, each new encounter could be the one that makes all the difference. Making a great first impression is incredibly important, and this is where your elevator pitch comes in. It's a brief, impactful introduction that covers who you are, what you do, why you're unique, and what your goals and ambitions are.

Your elevator pitch should last no longer than **30-60 seconds** to ensure you hold the listener's attention.

To craft a strong pitch, think about answering four key questions:

1. **Who Are You?**

   The success of your pitch starts with the opening. The first few words should immediately grab the listener's attention. What's the most important thing you want them to know about you? If possible, try to provide context that makes your pitch relevant to the listener. For example, you could talk about a common problem in the industry and how you could solve it. This sets the stage for what you offer.

Example:

"I know many media companies struggle to attract new customers because of the fierce competition. I specialise in business development for international media businesses."

2. **What Do You Do?**

   Once you've captured their attention, talk about your relevant experience and skills. This is where you can mention a recent project, your current or past roles, or any interesting achievements. Keep it brief but aim to include a detail that showcases your experience and level of expertise.

Example:
"I have a degree in media and five years of industry experience. In my current role, I've doubled lead generation in the last year by leveraging my network and understanding of what matters to buyers."

3. **Why Are You Unique?**
   Your pitch should explain what makes you stand out from others. These unique qualities are what set you apart and can be beneficial to the listener. Be sure to emphasise how your uniqueness can add value to the situation or solve a problem.

Example:
"I'm passionate about languages and taught myself German and French. This has allowed me to build a strong network in the European media industry, which has been instrumental in driving international sales."

4. **What Are Your Goals & Ambitions?**
   End your pitch by clearly stating your career goals and aligning them with what the listener is looking for. The key here is to be persuasive without being forceful. Consider ending your pitch with a call to action or a question that opens the door for further conversation.

Example:
"I'm looking for opportunities to further develop my career in international business development. I'm particularly interested in supporting companies expanding globally, like yours. I'd love to connect and discuss how I can help you attract new customers."

Crafting a great elevator pitch isn't something that happens overnight. It requires practice. The more you rehearse, the more **natural and authentic** your pitch will sound. It's always better to speak and improve your elevator pitch using your own words than writing it up front to have a natural lift. It's important to practice saying your pitch out loud, tweaking it until it feels right and flows smoothly. When you're comfortable with your pitch, you'll sound more confident and make a stronger impression on others.

Don't be too soon and too much! It will indicate that you are desperate. Develop it as a normal chat and use statements when you really need it.

Remember, your elevator pitch is not just about talking about your work or skills. It's about creating a connection. A great pitch does more than just convey your qualifications; it engages the listener and makes them want to know more about you. With a well-crafted elevator pitch, you'll be able to become memorable.

Power Circle

As human beings, we have evolved to thrive in communities. We are inherently social creatures who rely on connections to lead fulfilling lives. These communities can include family, friends, colleagues, club members, and even acquaintances. Each of these networks plays a vital role in shaping both our personal and professional journeys. In his book *Never Eat Alone: And Other Secrets to Success, One Relationship at a Time*, Keith Ferrazzi emphasises the importance of networking and building relationships early in your career. According to Ferrazzi, success is built not just on what you know but also on who you know and how you nurture those relationships.

Now, take a moment to think about the people in your network and how they can support your career goals. Building a "Power Circle" is a critical step in your career development. A Power Circle consists of trusted individuals who can help you grow and connect you to the right opportunities. This network can provide guidance, mentorship, referrals, and access to hidden job opportunities that you might otherwise miss.

In his book, *What Colour Is Your Parachute?* Richard Bolles discusses the concept of "Hidden Jobs." Many positions in the job market are never advertised because companies prefer to hire through their existing networks. This method reduces the cost and time of talent acquisition and management. Referrals from trusted connections play a significant role in this process, which is why many job opportunities remain hidden. By developing your Power Circle and nurturing relationships, you increase your chances of accessing these unadvertised roles, gaining a competitive edge in the job market. Therefore, building and maintaining a strong, supportive network is an essential strategy for career growth and success.

Steps to Build Your Power Circle

To maximize the potential of your network, identify the top five individuals in each category who can support your career aspirations. Among family and relatives, pinpoint those with valuable insights into your goals or connections in your target industry. From colleagues and mentors, select those who can offer mentorship, recommendations, or insider advice. Consider friends who are well-connected or already working in your field of interest. Lastly, within clubs and professional groups, focus on individuals who are active in industries or roles you aim to pursue. Prioritizing these connections helps you strategically leverage your network for guidance and opportunities.

1. **Map your network**

Richard Bolles emphasises that many job opportunities remain hidden, making networking an essential tool for accessing these roles. Building and maintaining relationships, along with leveraging informational interviews, can help uncover potential career paths. To start, reflect on your network, including family and relatives who understand your strengths and may have relevant connections, colleagues and mentors who can provide professional guidance and advocacy, friends who can offer fresh perspectives or referrals, and community or club members who share common interests or belong to professional organisations. Strategically engaging with these groups can unlock valuable insights and opportunities to support your career journey. Most often the answers to our questions, just a call away. It just a matter of identifying and making that call is all what you do.

2. Identify your top 5 contacts in each category

To maximize the potential of your network, identify the top five individuals in each category who can support your career aspirations. Among family and relatives, pinpoint those with valuable insights into your goals or connections in your target industry. From colleagues and mentors, select those who can offer mentorship, recommendations, or insider advice. Consider friends who are well-connected or already working in your field of interest. Lastly, within clubs and professional groups, focus on individuals who are active in industries or roles you aim to pursue. Prioritizing these connections helps you strategically leverage your network for guidance and opportunities.
Now, map these on a piece of paper and visualise your network.

3. Fostering the relationship & growing your circle

Fostering relationships within your network requires intentionality and reciprocity. Regularly reach out to your connections, show genuine interest in their lives, and express gratitude for their support. Offer value in return by sharing helpful resources, ideas, or opportunities, as networking thrives on mutual exchange. Seek advice, guidance, or mentorship, and tap into their networks by requesting referrals or introductions. Clearly communicate your goals and aspirations so they can effectively support you. Beyond your current circle, expand your network by attending professional events, joining online forums, and participating in industry-specific meetups to connect with new, like-minded individuals.

We most often meet people to "Use" our skills, knowledge and contact and do not feel those relationships honest and authentic. When you think about your inner circle, those relationships are ones that you must nurture and, hence, need to be authentic and consistent. It doesn't matter the quantity of contacts that you have but the quality of the contacts you have. Five good quality relationships that you maintain could change your life for the better than 1,000 loose connections. Hope these tips will help you in building those contacts. "Ten Thousand Coffee" is another online platform that connects mentors and HR professionals across the world that you might be interested in, but with a cost. It's always best to start from your own first.

Secrets of building strong relationships

I) Be Part of Others' Success

You don't have to be a master to cheer others on. Sometimes, simple encouragement can go a long way. However, the key is to ensure that your encouragement is honest and genuine. Dale Carnegie articulated this beautifully in his book *"How to Win Friends and Influence People"*. He wrote, *"You can make more friends in two months by becoming interested in other people than you can in two years by trying to get other people interested in you."*

Now, reflect on your most important contacts:
- What do they do?
- How can you support or add value to them?
- What do you genuinely admire about their work?

By showing sincere interest in others and celebrating their successes, you naturally create stronger, more meaningful connections.

II) Earn their trust

Trust is the foundation of any strong relationship. Throughout my life, I have employed the following principles to build trust within my network. Reflecting on these in your own life, you may find they resonate with your experiences and interactions.

a) Value long-term relationships over short-term gains

I focus on identifying individuals with whom I want to build trust and offer my support first, without expecting anything in return. This could include sharing useful contacts, resources, mentoring, or advice. Having a clear and positive intention transforms contacts into meaningful relationships. By nurturing these connections, I cultivate long-lasting bonds. At the same time, it's essential to recognize and respect personal boundaries in such interactions.

b) Be honest about what you can offer and deliver.

Building trust doesn't require fear of losing a relationship. Honesty and transparency create a solid foundation. Always keep your promises and aim to exceed expectations, but without overextending yourself. If you make a mistake, own up to it and take accountability—it demonstrates integrity and builds trust.

c) Communicate clearly and effectively.

Effective communication goes beyond mere information sharing. It involves your words, body language, gestures, and posture. As John Lees highlights in The Success Code, "It's not just about being yourself but remembering how you project yourself when you're at your best." Wearing confidence in every interaction enhances your communication and leaves a positive impression.

d) Avoid hidden agendas

Genuine care and respect for others build trust. Avoid using people for personal gain, and always respect their time, dignity, and efforts. If a relationship or interaction no longer holds value or authenticity, it's okay to distance yourself politely.

e) Embrace vulnerability

Perfection isn't achievable all the time and projecting it can create distance in relationships. Showing vulnerability, when appropriate and safe, demonstrates authenticity and strengthens connections.

f) Always strive to be helpful in any way you can.

A consistent effort to assist others—whether through advice, resources, or emotional support—creates a reputation of reliability and approachability

By demonstrating these behaviours, you can establish yourself as dependable, authentic, and trustworthy, creating a solid foundation for strong personal and professional relationships.

III) NAIL the Story

Kym Hamer shared a valuable framework to support initiating conversations and thinking about the other person's needs. Here's how to create impactful connections,

- Understanding their NEED.
- ASK Relevant Questions: Tailor your questions to their interest or goals. Use questions starting with "What," "Why," "When," or "How" encourage deeper engagement and understanding.
- INVITE Two-Way Conversations: Unlike products, people can reciprocate emotions. Build a connection through meaningful dialogue.
- Practice Active LISTENING: Listen to understand, not just to respond. In today's fast-paced world, listening is an underrated skill that can set you apart.

By genuinely listening and showing empathy, you can build trust and rapport quickly, turning initial conversations into long-lasting relationships.

Practising observations and listening effectively are key skills in identifying needs, asking relevant questions, and fostering engaging conversations. Often, asking the right question can serve as a conversation starter, addressing the exact problem your audience is facing.

For example, I might say in a conversation:
"I understand that choosing the right job can be a challenge. I work with young individuals, helping them identify career paths that align with their goals. What do you feel are the biggest barriers to making your decision?"

This approach invites the other person to open up about their struggles while positioning you as someone who can help guide them through the decision-making process. By being a good listener and asking insightful questions, you can not only initiate meaningful conversations but also create opportunities to provide value.

How this links to your career

Even during the early stages of your career, your network plays a pivotal role in opening doors for.

1. **Recommendations:**

Employers often request referees who can vouch for your abilities. Your network needs to understand your identity and strengths to provide strong recommendations.

2. **Opportunities**

Your first job often comes through your network, whether they recommend a position, refer you to an employer, or forward you an opportunity. To do this, your network needs to know:
- Who you are.
- What you do.
- What you're looking for.

3. **Guidance and Mentorship**

You'll need advice and direction throughout your career journey. Mentors, whether they are teachers, lecturers, friends, or professionals, can provide the clarity and support you need to grow.

How you can expand your network

Think about creative ways to broaden your connections. Here are some ideas:

- **Attend Events and Conferences:**
  Look for job fairs, exhibitions, or industry-specific meetups. For example, Sarah, who wanted to turn her passion for cake-making into a career, attended a wedding fair. She brought samples and photos, connected with wedding organisers, and landed her first orders.
- **Join Local Clubs and Societies:**
  Participate in walking groups, yoga classes, meditation groups, or hobby clubs. These activities not only boost your confidence but also expand your circle.
- **Leverage Local Newspapers and Community News:**
  Scan for companies expanding or hiring in your area. These could be potential employers.
- **Explore Your Neighbourhood:**
  Take a walk or drive through industrial estates or shopping centres. Note companies that align with your interests and skills.
- **Join Support Groups:**
  Look for national or local career support groups, alumni associations, or industry-specific forums to connect with like-minded individuals.

By following these steps, you can build meaningful relationships, foster trust, and open doors to career opportunities.

In summary

- Personal branding goes beyond just having a digital presence; it involves creating a purposeful and meaningful profile that reflects your career journey.
- To build an authentic personal brand, focus on three key elements: "Your Story," "Your Identity," and "Your Power Circle," all of which should be aligned.
- Your story, shaped by your experiences and values, forms the foundation of your personal brand, and it's important to own it with pride and authenticity.
- Equally, your identity should clearly reflect your unique qualities, helping others understand how you stand out from others in a professional setting.
- Your Power Circle, made up of family, friends, colleagues, and professional contacts, should read your story and feel that your identity is unique and memorable.
- By aligning your story, identity, and Power Circle, you can effectively craft a personal brand that resonates and propels your career forward.
- Drafting your own soundbites and elevator pitch are useful tools to clearly communicate who you are to your professional audience.
- Focusing on your strengths and connecting with others through authentic conversations helps build your personal brand and create a lasting, positive impression.

05

Creating your CV & Cover Letter

"Your CV is not just a document; it's an opportunity waiting to be recognised."

Breaking into the world of work is much like a seedling pushing through the soil. It must navigate not only the weight of the earth above but also compete with other seedlings vying for sunlight and space. To stand tall and claim its place, the seedling must harness every advantage it has.

At the end of reading this chapter, you will be able to,

- Identify the difference between a resume and a Curriculum Vitae (CV).
- Learn a step-by-step complete guide to building two types of main CVs.
- Develop your own powerful resume using the pro-tips shaped.
- Create a compelling cover letter that can be tailor-made to the job positions.
- Learn how to make your CV & cover letter ATS-friendly.

Curriculum Vitae and Resume?

One of the most important steps in job hunting, is building your *Curriculum Vitae* (CV) or Resume. Ideally, you should start thinking about your CV/resume as early as secondary school. That allows you to actively pursue qualifications and experiences to enrich your CV over time. People tend to use the terms CV and *resume* interchangeably. However, there are distinctions based on context and country. The below table offer you a very good overview of both.

Aspect	Curriculum Vitae (CV)	Resume
Purpose	Used primarily in academia, research, medical fields, or when applying for international careers.	Used in job applications in industries like business, tech, creative fields, and others.
Length	Typically, longer (2-4+ pages) as it provides a detailed overview of education, achievements, and experience.	Shorter (1-2 pages) focusing on the most relevant experience & Skills for the specific job.
Content	Comprehensive, including: - Academic background (degrees, certifications) - Research, publications, and presentations - Awards and honours - Teaching experience - Professional memberships - References	Concise, tailored to the job: - Contact information - Professional summary or objective - Work experience (relevant to the role) - Skills
Customization	Remains relatively static updated over time but not significantly altered for individual applications.	Highly customizable tailored to each job by focusing on relevant experience and keywords.
Region	Common in Europe, Asia, Africa, and academia globally.	Common in the U.S., Canada, and business sectors worldwide.
Focus	Emphasises academic achievements and a complete professional history.	Highlights skills and achievements most relevant to the specific role.
Tone	Formal and detailed.	Professional but concise and dynamic.

When to use which document
- Use a CV when:
    - Applying for academic, research, or medical roles.
    - Required by international employers (especially in countries where CVs are standard).
- Use a Resume when:
    - Applying for jobs in corporate, creative, or technical industries.
    - You need a quick, impactful summary of your qualifications.

A CV provides a full history of your academic and professional background, while a Resume is a concise, tailored document designed to demonstrate your suitability for a specific role. Understanding the distinction helps you present your qualifications effectively in different professional contexts.

Here in this book, I refer CV as a common document which can be tailormade to diverse contexts and requirements.

Building your Ideal CV

Think about the part you most struggle with when writing your own CV? How confident do you feel about what needs to be included in a CV? Do you think there is anything missing from your own CV? You will get all the answers here.

There are two kinds of CVs.
Let's dive deep into each.

Regardless of the type of CV you choose the most important thing to remember is that "Every word counts." On average, employers spend just 7 seconds reviewing a CV, so it's crucial to convey the most relevant information for the opportunity. Your CV should be simple, concise, and tailored to meet the specific demands of the employer. By doing so, you significantly reduce the chances of it being discarded.

In this context, identifying the type of CV that aligns with the job and its requirements is vital. A well-matched CV increases your chances of making a strong impression and progressing to the next stage of the hiring process.

1) Skills Based CVs.

Nowadays, skills-based CVs are gaining popularity in the industry as employers increasingly prioritize skills over experience. People are being hired for their technical and soft skills, which have become critical in the job market. For early-career professionals, this type of CV is an excellent choice to highlight transferable skills, making their profiles more appealing to potential employers. **[Template 01 & 2]**

A skills-based CV emphasises the specific abilities you possess that are relevant to the sector or role you're targeting.

For example, if you're applying for a UX/UI Designer position but lack extensive work experience, this CV format is ideal for showcasing your skills effectively. It allows you to highlight your capabilities through examples and projects you've worked on, which is especially useful for individuals with freelance or gig experience.

Nowadays, many young professionals engage in gig work or freelancing across various platforms, which provides an excellent opportunity to showcase your expertise. By emphasizing relevant projects, you can leave a strong and lasting impression on potential employers.

Pro tip: The key to creating a compelling skills-based CV is to thoroughly review the job description, identify the most relevant skills required for the position, and tailor your examples to align with those skills. This approach ensures your CV is focused and impactful, increasing your chances of securing an interview.

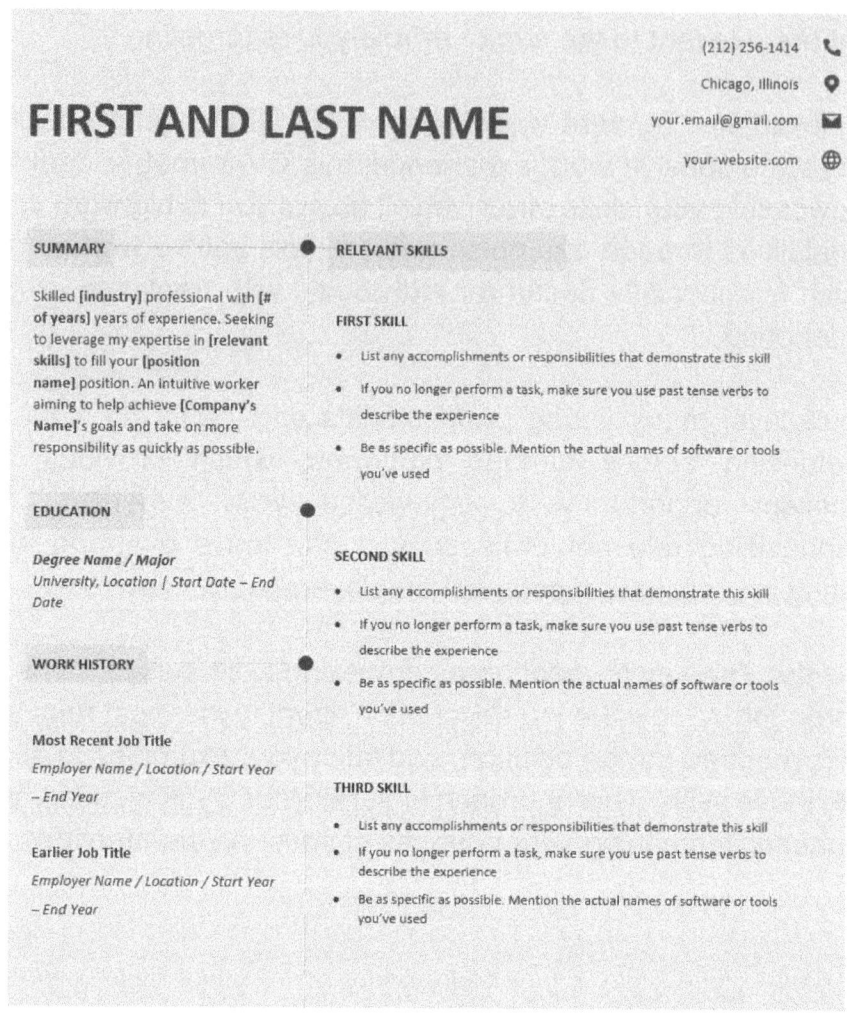

Figure 12-Skills Based CV-Template 01 - resumegenius.com

YOUR NAME

Phone | Email | Location (City, State, ZIP)
Online Portfolio/Professional Website (Optional)

PROFESSIONAL SUMMARY

2-3 sentences or 2-3 bullet points that include your years of professional experience, accomplishments, top skills and strengths as they relate to the position and what you're looking for in your next role.

RELEVANT SKILLS

Include three-to-four bullets that have as many specific and quantifiable examples as possible.

[Skill #1]
- List an achievement and/or work experience that portrays evidence of how you used the skill in your work history.

[Skill #2]
- List an achievement and/or work experience that portrays evidence of how you used the skill in your work history.

[Skill #3]
- List an achievement and/or work experience that portrays evidence of how you used the skill in your work history.

EXPERIENCE

Title   **Start Date - End Date (Current)**
Company Name, Location
- (Action verb) + what you did (more detail) + reason, outcome or quantified results
- (Action verb) + what you did (more detail) + reason, outcome or quantified results
- (Action verb) + what you did (more detail) + reason, outcome or quantified results

Title   **Start Date - End Date**
Company Name, Location
- (Action verb) + what you did (more detail) + reason, outcome or quantified results
- (Action verb) + what you did (more detail) + reason, outcome or quantified results
- (Action verb) + what you did (more detail) + reason, outcome or quantified results

EDUCATION

Degree Type, Major (if applicable) | **Month/Year of Completion**
Institution Name

CERTIFICATIONS
- **[Certification]**, [Certifying organization] - [Year earned]

AWARDS/RECOGNITIONS/VOLUNTEER WORK - (OPTIONAL)
- Award, recognition or volunteer work   Date
- Award, recognition or volunteer work   Date

Figure 13 -Skills Based CV -Template 2 -Source :(Indeed,2024)

2) Chronological CVs

Chronological CVs are the most common format used to present a clear timeline of your experience and qualifications to potential employers. This type of CV arranges your work history in reverse chronological order, starting with your most recent role.

You can customize the structure based on the job description, ensuring that every section is strategically utilized to highlight your suitability for the role. To help you maximize its impact,

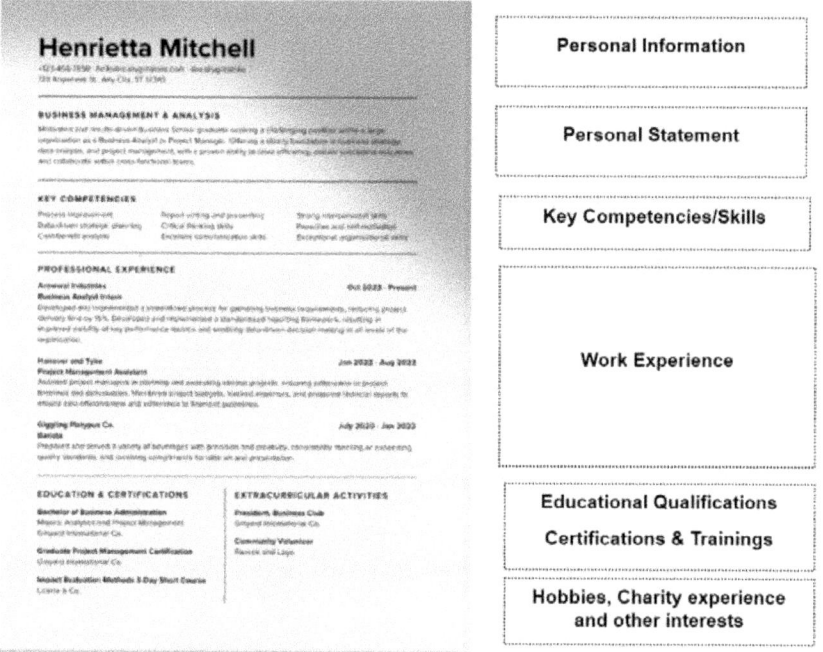

Here are the most used sections of a chronological CV, with detailed explanations for each:

Personal Information

Include your name, professional email address, phone number, LinkedIn profile (if applicable), and location. Ensure this section is easy to read and updated.

Do not use a Photo in your CV as most organisations globally discourage this as it can invite bias.

If you have a long name, use the most preferred part of your name and surname.
Avoid using fancy names for your email and create a new professional email address to include in your CV. It is also encouraged to use the country and the name of the city and advised not to include the full address on the CV.

If you have a specific blog that can link to your profile or website, if it adds value to your portfolio, it is better to mention it here with the links.

Ex.

Marie Sharp

Your town | Your mobile number | Your email address | Your LinkedIn/Twitter/Instagram link

Personal Statement

A summary of who you are, your key strengths, and what you're seeking in your next role. This section should be tailored to the specific job and provide a snapshot of your suitability.

It should ideally be very short and use 50-150 words or 3-4 concise statements: the shorter the better. Here are some guides to developing a compelling personal statement. Follow through each step and write one single sentence to cover the instructions.

Step-by-Step Guide

Step 1: Introduce yourself and highlight your identity.
- Example 1: *A qualified, detail-oriented, and organised bookkeeping professional currently completing an internship.*
- Example 2: *A motivated and ambitious graduate specialising in data science.*

Step 2: Demonstrate your skills and value to potential employers.

- Example 1: *Proficient in financial transactions, reconciling accounts, and using accounting software with a focus on accuracy and confidentiality.*
- Example 2: *Skilled in analysing datasets, creating dashboards, and effectively collaborating within teams to achieve results.*

Step 3: Include key achievements or experiences.

- Example 1: *Experience managing accounts payable/receivable and preparing financial reports with compliance.*
- Example 2: *Ranked among the top 3 data science projects of 2024 for developing use cases and innovative dashboards.*

Step 4: Summarize aspirations and align with the job.

- Example 1: *I am eager to contribute to an entry-level bookkeeping role and support your finance team's success.*

- Example 2: *I aspire to expand my professional exposure by contributing to impactful projects in a forward-looking organisation.*

Compiled Example

Example 1: Bookkeeping Professional
A qualified, detail-oriented, and accurate bookkeeping candidate with hands-on experience from an internship. Proficient in managing financial transactions, reconciling accounts, and using accounting software, I have honed skills in accuracy, confidentiality, and organisation. My experience includes handling accounts payable/receivable and payroll support while maintaining compliance with protocols. I am eager to contribute my analytical skills and commitment to accuracy to your finance team.

Example 2: Data Science Graduate
A qualified and ambitious graduate specialising in data science. With skills in data analysis, dashboard development, and project management, I collaborate effectively to deliver results. Recognised for my work as a top 3 data science graduate project of 2024, I aspire to gain industry exposure and expand my professional development through impactful projects in an innovative organisation.

Pro Tips
a) **Tailor for relevance:** Customize each personal statement using keywords from the job description.
b) **Keep it simple:** Use clear language without jargon, ensuring it's easy for non-experts to understand.
c) **Focus on readability:** Be concise yet impactful, avoiding lengthy or redundant phrases.

Work Experience:

To optimize the experience section of your CV and make it stand out, follow these guidelines:

Identify Relevant Roles:
If you're an early career professional, include any internships or part-time roles that align with your career aspirations. Focus on roles that match the job you're applying for. For experienced professionals, highlight roles within the last 10 years, particularly those relevant to the position you're targeting.

Start with Recent Experience:
Always list your most recent role first. If you're still working in the position, use "To date."

Introduce Your Job:
Write 1-2 lines summarizing what you were hired to do. If applicable, mention any promotions or advancements and provide key details such as team size, budget, or scope of responsibility.

Link Responsibilities to Achievements:

When detailing your experience, it's essential to differentiate between responsibilities and achievements. Responsibilities are the tasks and duties that you're expected to perform as part of your role. Achievements, however, highlight the impact of your work and the tangible results you've delivered. Here's how to reflect on your experience more effectively:

- **Were you given extra responsibilities at work? If yes, what did that lead to?**
  Think about how taking on additional tasks helped improve your workflow, expanded your skillset, or positioned you for career advancement.
- **Have you ever been promoted or publicly recognised for your work?**
  Recognition, whether formal or informal, is a strong indicator of your performance and contribution to the company.
- **Have you ever won any work-related awards?**
  If you received accolades or awards for your work, this is a significant achievement to highlight, as it shows external validation of your impact.
- **Have you exceeded targets or goals?**
  Going beyond the expectations of your role can demonstrate a commitment to excellence. Be specific about what targets were exceeded and how.
- **Have you helped a customer or colleague overcome a problem?**
  Problem-solving is a highly valued skill. If you've solved challenges, whether for clients or colleagues, mention the outcome and the positive impact it had.
- **Have you ever delivered exceptional customer service?**
  Going above and beyond for clients or customers showcases your dedication to their satisfaction, which is crucial in any industry.
- **Have you ever improved systems, processes, or workflows?**
  Process improvements are a key achievement. Show how your contributions helped make your workplace more efficient, cost-effective, or productive.

Key Responsibilities vs Key Achievements:

Key Responsibilities are typically tasks that are expected of you as part of your role, such as managing daily operations, following established procedures, or maintaining records.
Key Achievements are the measurable results or positive changes you brought about. These are the milestones or outcomes that make you stand out to future employers.

For example:
- **Key Responsibility**: Managed an office filing system.
- **Key Achievement**: Introduced a new naming convention and an online filing system, making it 30% faster to locate and share documents across a team of 25.

By focusing on achievements, you demonstrate your value to potential employers and show that you can contribute to their success in a meaningful way. This distinction is what will make your CV stand out.

Instead of simply listing responsibilities, link them to specific achievements. This approach shows how you made an impact in your role and demonstrates your skills. Use bullet points to highlight your key achievements, and always start each bullet point with a strong action verb. Focus on measurable results, such as improvements, savings, or efficiencies.

Here's an example to illustrate:

Data Analyst Intern
XYZ Corporation | June 2023 – August 2023
Hired to assist the data team in analysing sales trends, supporting the development of dashboards, and conducting market research.

- **Analysed** customer data to identify purchasing trends, leading to a 15% improvement in targeted marketing strategies.
- **Streamlined** data collection processes, reducing processing time by 20% and enhancing the accuracy of reports.
- **Collaborated** with cross-functional teams to develop a dashboard that visually represented key performance indicators, increasing team efficiency by 30%.

In this example, the responsibilities (data analysis, supporting dashboard development) are linked to specific achievements (improvements, reductions, and collaborations). The action verbs "analysed," "streamlined," and "collaborated" give each bullet point more impact. Make sure to use relevant action verbs and focus on the results of your work to make your CV stand out.

A list of Keywords you can use can be found here (Source: Skillshub.Com)

List of active words

Use this list to start each bullet point on your CV. These words will help you to think about your achievements and help you to make the most impact from each of them.

Accumulated	Aligned	Arranged	Analysed
Accomplished	Anticipated	Assumed	Adopted
Budgeted	Balanced	Brainstormed	Battled
Compiled	Championed	Calculated	Conceptualised
Changed	Captured	Commenced	Conducted
Delivered	Dispatched	Dedicated	Displayed
Explained	Explored	Envisioned	Evaluated
Formulated	Finalised	Fine-tuned	Fulfilled
Generated	Gained	Gathered	Gauged
Handled	Heightened	Hunted	Highlighted
Inspected	Influenced	Identified	Inspired
Launched	Listened	Lobbied	Listed
Managed	Mentored	Motivated	Monitored
Manufactured	Marketed	Minimised	Maximised
Negotiated	Notified	Neutralised	Nurtured
Optimised	Overhauled	Outsourced	Overcame
Promoted	Practised	Persevered	Produced
Polished	Probed	Protected	Performed
Released	Rectified	Repaired	Raised
Revitalised	Revealed	Reshaped	Reached
Spearheaded	Sold	Sharpened	Secured
Surpassed	Succeeded	Specialised	Stimulated
Translated	Targeted	Terminated	Theorised
Undertook	Uncovered	Unveiled	Utilised
Volunteered	Valued	Verified	Visualised
Won	Wrote	Withdrew	Widened

Figure 14 - List of Keywords to use in CVs.

Education & Qualifications

List your academic qualifications in reverse chronological order, including the institution name, degree or certification earned, and the completion date. Prioritize the qualifications most relevant to the job you are applying for. If you are pursuing an academic career or have a final year project or thesis that directly relates to the industry, mention the topic to highlight your expertise in that area. In today's fast-paced work environment, continuous professional development is vital. Therefore, include a section on relevant certifications, licenses, or training courses you've completed to demonstrate your ongoing commitment to learning and keeping your skills up to date.

Key Skills

While a skills section is not always necessary in a chronological CV, it can be highly beneficial for showcasing your abilities quickly, especially if they align with the job description. Place this section after your personal statement or education if you are not using a skills-based CV. To optimize this section, carefully review the job description to identify the most critical skills/T shaped skills required, then reflect on your own experiences and highlight your skills using relevant keywords. For each skill, include a brief sentence that demonstrates how you've applied or developed that skill, ideally linking them to transferable skills gained from your hobbies or past experiences (as discussed in Chapter 2).

6. Additional Information:

Use this section to include any awards, language proficiencies, volunteer experience, or hobbies that are relevant to the role. If these aspects haven't been covered in the skills section, this is the perfect place to include them. When presenting this information, make sure to relate it to how it adds value to the position you're applying for, showing how these experiences contribute to your suitability for the job. Highlight any achievements or personal development that could bring extra value to your future employer.

How can you make hobbies and interests relevant to the job role?

When writing your CV or preparing for an interview, it's important to show how your hobbies and interests align with the skills and qualities required in the role. Think about the transferable skills you've developed through your hobbies and how they can be applied in the workplace. As discussed in Chapter 2, transferable skills are abilities that can be used in various roles and industries, and they can often be gained or honed through personal interests.

Here's how you can elaborate on your hobbies to make them relevant to the job:

Your Hobby	How You Can Elaborate in Your CV
Team Sports (e.g., Football, Basketball)	*Demonstrates teamwork, communication, leadership, and the ability to collaborate towards a common goal.*
Volunteering for a Charity	*Highlights empathy, social responsibility, and project management skills, as well as the ability to work with diverse teams.*
Blogging or Content Creation	*Shows creativity, writing skills, digital literacy, and ability to communicate effectively with an audience.*
Travelling	*Shows adaptability, curiosity, cultural awareness, and the ability to navigate new challenges.*
Public Speaking	*Displays strong communication, confidence, presentation, and leadership skills.*
Photography	*Illustrates attention to detail, creativity, and technical skills, including proficiency with design software and image editing.*
Learning a New Language	*Demonstrates commitment to personal growth, cultural awareness, and communication skills in a diverse work environment.*
Gardening or DIY Projects	*Shows problem-solving skills, patience, and the ability to handle tasks independently.*
Chess	*Highlights strategic thinking, planning, and decision-making abilities.*
Fitness or Marathon Training	*Displays discipline, time management, and a commitment to long-term goals.*

By framing your hobbies in this way, you show potential employers that you bring a diverse range of skills to the table beyond just your formal education or work experience. This can make you a more well-rounded and attractive candidate for the role.

How can I make use of My CV/Resume?

Once you prepare your CV most important and crucial part of the process is done. Then, you need to use this tool to effectively search for your ideal career opportunity. You can share your CV with.

I)   Your friends and family who have contacts and willing to support
II) Local job centre
III) Recruitment agencies (either online or face-to-face)
IV) Job websites
V)   Directly with employers (in person or online)
VI) Newspapers – social media – Word of mouth

Recruitment Process

Different companies follow unique recruitment approaches, with some outsourcing parts or all of their recruitment process while others manage it in-house. Regardless of the method, most recruitment processes start with publishing a job advertisement and calling for CVs. Candidates are typically required to either upload a pre-prepared CV or fill out details in an in-house recruitment portal. Here's an overview of how the process unfolds and tips for creating an ATS-friendly CV:

Stages of Recruitment:

1. **Job Advertisement and CV Submission:**

Job advertisements are typically posted on job boards, company websites, professional platforms like LinkedIn and Indeed, or through recruitment agencies. Candidates submit their CVs in various formats, either by uploading them or using tailored application portals. However, as mentioned earlier, many candidates fall into the trap of the "spray and pray" approach, submitting the same CV to multiple job listings without tailoring it for each role. This often leads to immediate rejection, even if the candidate has the right qualifications and experience.

Employers often receive thousands of applications and need a way to filter the right candidates. They begin by looking for basic qualifications, visa status, and any special conditions that help narrow down the pool. Errors in the CV or a lack of customisation can lead to an immediate rejection. To stand out, it's crucial to tailor your CV for each job application, ensuring it aligns with the specific role's requirements.

Additionally, it's essential to update your CV on platforms like LinkedIn and job portals at least every two weeks, using a file name under 16 characters. This will prompt the algorithm to recognise it as a new version and push notifications for fresh job opportunities. Using relevant keywords for skills on your LinkedIn profile also helps attract the right job opportunities, making it easier for recruiters to find you.

2. **Automated Filtering via ATS (Applicant Tracking Systems):**

Many companies use ATS to filter CVs based on keywords extracted from the job description. This system scans submitted CVs and cover letters for compatibility with the job's requirements, significantly reducing manual effort. Understanding how ATS works is crucial for applicants.

3. **Manual Review by Recruitment Teams:**

CVs that pass the ATS filtering process are then reviewed by recruitment teams for:
  - **Prerequisites:** Checking eligibility, such as visa status.
  - **Shortlisting:** Selecting candidates for further evaluation.

4. **Further Evaluation:**

Depending on the volume of applications, companies may:
  - Conduct **assessment centres** or tests to evaluate skills and suitability.
  - Proceed with **multiple interview stages**, starting with phone/video screenings and advancing to panel or technical interviews.

Creating an ATS-Friendly CV:

1. **Use Keywords:**
   Identify key terms from the job description and incorporate them naturally into your CV. Focus on:
   - Required skills.
   - Relevant qualifications.
   - Specific tools or technologies mentioned in the job description.
2. **Simple Formatting:**
   Avoid overly creative designs that might confuse ATS software. Use:
   - Standard fonts like Arial, Calibri, or Times New Roman.
   - Clear headings (e.g., Work Experience, Education, Skills).
   - Bulleted lists to showcase accomplishments.
3. **Avoid Graphics and Tables:**
   ATS may struggle to read non-text elements. Stick to plain text for optimal compatibility.
4. **Use Standard Section Titles:**
   Sections like "Experience," "Education," and "Skills" are universally recognised by ATS.
5. **File Format:**
   Submit your CV in the format specified in the job posting. When in doubt, PDF or Word documents are usually safe choices.
6. **Customization:**
   Tailor your CV for each role by aligning your qualifications and experiences with the job description. Highlight your most relevant achievements and skills.

By following these guidelines, your CV has a higher chance of passing through ATS filters and get shortlisted.

Building a Strong Cover Letter

A cover letter is a crucial part of any job application, serving as your introduction to the employer. It provides an opportunity to make a strong first impression, highlight why you're the ideal candidate, and demonstrate your interest in the role. Here's how a well-crafted cover letter can set you apart:

- **Creates a Positive First Impression**: Demonstrates your effort and attention to detail.

- **Supplements Your CV**: Allows you to present your unique qualities and explain why you're a strong fit before the employer delves into your CV.

- **Engages the Employer**: Increases the likelihood they'll review your CV.

- **Showcases Motivation**: Explains your interest in the role and the company.

- **Highlights Key Strengths**: Bring attention to your accomplishments or skills that may not be fully elaborated in your CV.

Key Elements of a Strong Cover Letter

1. **Your Contact Details:**
   Include your name, email address, phone number, and LinkedIn profile (if applicable) at the top. This ensures the employer can easily reach you.

2. **Recruiter's Name and Address:**
   If the recruiter's name and company address are provided in the job advert, include them. When only the name is available, a quick search (e.g., LinkedIn or company website) can provide additional details. If uncertain about the name, avoid guessing, better to use a general salutation than risk addressing the wrong person.

Proper Salutation:
Personalize the greeting wherever possible. For example:

- "Dear [Recruiter's First Name]"
- "Dear [Title and Last Name], e.g., Mrs. Smith"
  Avoid generic greetings like "Dear Sir/Madam" or "To Whom It May Concern" unless absolutely necessary.

3. **Purpose of the Application:**
   Explain why you are applying for the role. Be specific about what excites you about the position and why you want to work for this company.

4. **Overview of Experience and Fit:**
   Provide a concise summary of your professional background, skills, and achievements, emphasizing how they align with the job requirements.

5. **Address Career Gaps (If Applicable):**
   If you have employment gaps, briefly explain them in a professional and positive tone. For example, "During my career break, I pursued certifications in [field], which have enhanced my expertise in [relevant area]."

6. **Demonstrate Knowledge About the Company:**
   Show that you've researched the company. Highlight specific initiatives, values, or recent achievements that resonate with you. For example:
   - "I was particularly inspired by [Company's Initiative/Project], which aligns with my passion for [related field]."

7. **Close on a Confident and Proactive Note:**
   End with a compelling tone. Avoid vague phrases like "I hope to hear from you." Instead, be assertive:
   - "I look forward to discussing how my skills and experiences can contribute to [Company's Name]. I am available at your convenience and can be reached at [contact information]."

8. **Tailor It for Each Role:**
   Customize your cover letter to align with the specific job description, using keywords and highlighting relevant experiences.

9. **Keep It Clear, Concise, and Error-Free:**
   Avoid lengthy paragraphs or overly complex language. Proofread to ensure it's free of grammatical and spelling errors.

Sample Cover Letter Structure

[Your Name]
[Your Address]
[City, State, ZIP]
[Your Email Address]
[Your Phone Number]

[Date]
[Recruiter's Name]
[Company Name]
[Company Address]

Dear [Recruiter's Name],

Opening Paragraph/s: State the purpose of your application, referencing the role and expressing enthusiasm for the position. Briefly mention what attracted you to the company. If someone or some program recommended the position, you can mention those as an opening.

Middle Paragraph(s): Provide a concise overview of your experience and achievements, linking them to the role. Mention specific skills, projects, or successes relevant to the position. If applicable, explain any career gaps or transitions. Highlight areas that you could not mention in the CV but are a good example to showcase your fit.

Closing Paragraph: Summarize why you are the ideal candidate and express your eagerness to contribute to the company. End with a proactive statement about your availability for further discussion and provide your contact details.

Sincerely,
[Your Name]

By incorporating these elements and tailoring each letter to the job, you'll craft a compelling and professional cover letter that maximizes your chances of securing an interview.

It's important to remember that your CV and cover letter must be customized for each job description. Ensure that you include relevant keywords from the job description to increase the

chances of your application being noticed by both recruiters and Applicant Tracking Systems (ATS). Tailoring your application materials not only highlights your fit for the role but also demonstrates your commitment and attention to detail.

In summary

- It is crucial to understand the difference between a CV and a resume, as well as their meanings in different contexts.
- Selecting the right CV type; whether skills-based or chronological-based on your role and experience level is key to clearly showcasing your eligibility.
- Crafting each section of your CV carefully and concisely, while presenting your best self and aligning it with the job role, is vital in creating a powerful CV.
- The skills section is particularly important, and outlining your T-shaped skills clearly can make a significant impact.
- Different employers have varying recruitment processes, and understanding these differences is essential when approaching them.
- Building an ATS-friendly CV is also critical for improving your chances of getting shortlisted and noticed.
- A cover letter complements your CV by elaborating on details beyond its scope, and it should be tailored to both the role and the company.
- Having these tools in place will help you stand out in the competitive job mark

06

Turning Rejections into an Opportunity

Imagine a tiny seedling breaking through the soil for the first time. The sunlight feels within reach, but harsh winds, rocks, and shadows quickly remind it of the challenges ahead. These obstacles may seem like setbacks or even rejection, pushing the seedling back into the dirt. Yet, with the right mindset, the seedling doesn't give up; it adapts, stretches its roots deeper, and grows stronger. Just like the seedling, every rejection you face is an opportunity to build resilience, refine your path, and rise above the challenges, thriving in ways you never thought possible.

At the end of Reading this Chapter, you will be able to,

- Identify how to make 3 contact approach to make a referral
- Understand how to clearly position a deliverable
- Evaluate rejections to turn them into opportunities.
- Use feedback to make the job search effective.

Most candidates upload their CVs and passively wait for an interview invitation, often overlooking the highly competitive nature of the job market. In this "red ocean" scenario, where many candidates vie for the same position, rejection doesn't necessarily mean you're not qualified; it simply means others may stand out in different ways. Moreover, companies typically have limited vacancies to fill despite the volume of applications. This is your life and opportunity, so you can't leave it to luck. Take control and own the process.

Here's how to stand out, step by step:

The Three-Contact Approach

a) Getting your referral

Before applying, start researching potential connections, particularly on LinkedIn. Explore the company page and identify people with shared backgrounds, such as alumni from your university, colleagues from previous jobs, or individuals with similar interests or volunteering experiences. Aim to find 2-3 people with commonalities and connect with them. Avoid directly asking for a job; instead, seek information and advice.

> **Sample Message:**
> *"Hi [Name],*
> *I noticed that we both studied at [University] in [Year].*
> *It's inspiring to see you excelling in [Field]. How have you been?*
> *Thanks,*
> *[Your Name]"*

This approach is almost certain to elicit a response. Continue the conversation by exchanging valuable information and keeping your profile visible and engaging. Perhaps introduce a useful resource or a mutual connection to add value to the relationship. After building rapport, follow up after a few days to discuss job opportunities.

> **Sample Message:**
> *"Hi [Name],*
> *I came across a job posting for a [Product Manager] position at your company. After speaking with you, I feel the company's culture and environment align well with my aspirations. What are your thoughts on this opportunity?*
> *Thanks,*
> *[Your Name]"*

Your contact is likely to provide guidance or direct you to someone relevant. Based on the conversation, you can politely ask if they might refer you for the position. Many companies offer incentives for employee referrals, making this beneficial for both parties.

By taking these proactive steps, you elevate your application above others and significantly improve your chances of success. Congratulations! By making a referral, you make the first contact with your potential employer.

b) Follow up to inform

Many technical jobs at reputed companies require applicants to complete lengthy and detailed application forms. It's common for candidates to spend several days completing these applications. Interestingly, only 4 out of 10 applicants finish the entire process. By simply completing the application, you already stand out among the competition. However, many candidates give up opportunities because companies take longer to respond, which is not a reasonable excuse to quit.

For reputed companies, job candidates are treated as their customers. A poor candidate experience can significantly harm the company's reputation and bottom line. For example, Virgin Media once estimated that bad candidate experiences cost them £4.4 million annually, as poorly treated candidates cancelled their subscriptions. While company hiring processes may sometimes be slow and inefficient due to ongoing business challenges, hiring managers are eager to find potential candidates to meet their targets. Following up on your application demonstrates enthusiasm and helps hiring managers identify you among the many random applications in their database.

A recent survey found that 48% of candidates upload their CVs online, while 35% email their CVs directly to hiring managers. If you can find the contact information of a hiring manager, emailing them directly is one of the most effective ways to get noticed. Employee referrals are also highly effective in many cases. Regardless of how you apply, following up on your application within 6–8 days is crucial.

When reaching out, avoid explicitly asking for the job. Instead, focus on showing your passion for the role and updating the hiring manager about your latest projects or qualifications to reinforce why you are a top candidate.

Here's an example of a professional follow-up email:

Subject: *Follow-Up on Application for [Well-Being Champion]*
Dear [Hiring Manager's Name],

It's a pleasure connecting with you. I recently applied for the [Well-Being Champion] position at your company. I am keen to join because of your unique company culture, which I explored through your recent article published in [Magazine Name]. At my current company, I pioneered the "Thrive" program to promote happiness at work. I am eager to contribute similarly to your organisation. Please let me know if you require any additional information regarding my application or CV.

Thank you for your time.
[Your Name]

Sending such a follow-up email increases your chances of being noticed. What are the possible outcomes?

1. **The company is still in the process of shortlisting candidates.** By following up, you get noticed.
2. **A candidate has already been selected.** Even if the position is filled, your effort isn't wasted. Companies often add strong candidates to a "Future Reference" or "Potential" folder for upcoming opportunities.
3. **You get invited to the next stage of the hiring process.**

There's nothing to lose. When you find an ideal opportunity, don't let it slip away. Showing enthusiasm not only enhances your chances but also reflects your loyalty and commitment to the company.

c) Follow up to Show you are passionate

If you don't receive a response after your second follow-up, the timing of your third contact depends on their latest communication. If they provided a timeline, follow up the day after it passes. Otherwise, wait another 5–8 business days.

Here's an example of a third follow-up email:

Subject: Follow-Up on [Position Name] Application

Dear [Hiring Manager's Name],

I applied for the [Position Name] position a few weeks ago and wanted to let you know that I remain highly interested in the role. Please let me know if you require any additional details or clarification regarding my application.

Thank you for your time.
[Your Name]

Alternatively, if you've received another job offer but still prefer this company, communicate the situation politely:

Subject: *Update on [Position Name] Application*
Dear [Hiring Manager's Name],
I applied for the [Position Name] position a few weeks ago and wanted to reiterate my interest in joining your company. I have recently progressed in the interview process for another opportunity in the same industry. However, I would prefer to proceed with your company if possible. Please let me know if additional information is needed to expedite your decision-making process.

Thank you for your time.
[Your Name]

Following this three-contact approach increases the likelihood of being remembered and considered. Always follow up after sending your CV and even after your first interview. Consistent, thoughtful communication showcases your professionalism and genuine interest in the company.

Creating a Deliverable

One way to make your three contacts with a potential employer memorable and irresistible is by providing them with a **"deliverable."**

What is a deliverable? It's a tangible demonstration of your expertise and value tailored to the job role. Every position comes with high expectations, and you can use your knowledge and experience to showcase how you meet them. For example, if your recent certification equipped you with new skills or exposed you to a relevant case study, you could create and share your ideas on how to address an upcoming company project or solve a specific problem they might face.

This approach not only highlights your ability to think critically but also demonstrates initiative and creativity. You can present your deliverable in various formats; such as a document, video, infographic, or slide deck; designed to spark curiosity and make them want to learn more about you.

For instance, during my mentoring journey, I've encountered candidates who successfully applied this method. By sharing a well-thought-out deliverable, they stood out from the competition and showcased the unique value they could bring to the organisation. This proactive approach often led to meaningful engagement with the hiring team, and, in some cases, job offers.

Taking this extra step positions you as a forward-thinking professional and makes your application unforgettable.

Turning Rejection to an opportunity

In life, not everything comes easily. It's a journey filled with obstacles, objections, and rejections; this is especially true for job applications. Even sending rejection emails can be a difficult task for companies. They often know you're a good candidate but may face limited opportunities or internal bottlenecks. So, how can you stand out amidst the chaos?

Research shows that 8 out of 10 candidates are discouraged from applying to a company again if they didn't receive feedback on a previous application. This highlights the importance of maintaining a positive impression even after a rejection. Recruitment processes are expensive, and companies aim to save costs wherever possible. If you've made a strong impression using the "three-contact" approach, you'll likely be remembered for future opportunities or sudden openings. Building and nurturing professional connections through existing networks further strengthens your standing with the company.

Receiving a rejection email can be disheartening. It's natural to feel disappointed, demotivated, or even begin to doubt yourself. However, you shouldn't let these feelings overshadow your opportunity to leave a lasting impression. Avoid replying immediately. Take some time to process your emotions and let the initial disappointment subside. Once you've regained composure, respond thoughtfully to acknowledge their email and their challenges. Reassure them of your enthusiasm for future roles and express your eagerness to be considered for upcoming opportunities.

If you've already gone through the interview process, use your response to appreciate their efforts and professionalism while sharing any valuable feedback you gained during the interview.

Few candidates take the initiative to respond graciously to a rejection. Doing so not only demonstrates your resilience but also sets you apart from others.

This approach could turn what seems like a closed door into an open window of opportunity. Your professionalism and persistence might lead the company to refer you for another position or keep you in mind for future roles.

Here is a sample email.

Subject: *Thank You for the Opportunity*

Dear [Hiring Manager's Name],

Thank you for informing me about the outcome of my application for the [Position Name] role. While I am, of course, disappointed by the decision, I truly appreciate the opportunity to get interviewed and learn more about [Company Name]. It was a pleasure speaking with you and your team.

I would be grateful if you could share any feedback on my application or interview performance.

Understanding your perspective would be invaluable in helping me refine my skills and prepare for future opportunities.

I remain impressed by [specific aspect of the company, e.g., "your commitment to innovation" or "the supportive company culture"], and I hope to have the chance to contribute to your team in the future. Please do keep me in mind for any roles that align with my skills and experience.

Thank you again for your time and consideration. I wish you and the team continued success.

Best regards,
[Your Full Name]
[Your Contact Information]

Remember, persistence pays off. Stand firm, stay positive, and keep pushing forward—because success often comes to those who persevere.

Take the Gift

Job searching in the early stages of your career is an essential part of your professional development. Think of it as career training-each application and interaction with a company helps you practice and refine your approach. If you commit to the process and stay consistent, you'll master it over time. Trust the journey.

As part of this process, you may receive valuable feedback on your CV, interview performance, or the reasons you weren't selected for a position. Take advantage of these moments to clarify any doubts in a friendly and professional tone. Make a list of the insights you gather and analyse them thoroughly. Reflect on the skills you may need to develop, areas that require more practice, and improvements to implement before your next opportunity arises.

Treat feedback as a **gift**; a tool for both personal and professional growth. By embracing it with a positive mindset, you can transform constructive criticism into actionable steps that pave the way for future success. Most importantly, believe in yourself and your ability to improve. This mindset will not only help you grow but will also set you apart as someone who values learning and resilience.

In Summary

- Winning your dream job at your desired company requires more than luck-it's about combining planning with opportunity.
- Building connections within your network can help you create effective referrals, increasing your chances of success.
- Following up with the company 6-8 days after the interview and seeking feedback is crucial for securing future opportunities.
- Sharing updates or a relevant deliverable is another great way to demonstrate your interest and stay memorable.
- Additionally, reaching out to the hiring manager through a well-written message or a thoughtful call can leave a lasting impression and strengthen your candidacy.

07

Mastering Interviews

"Is doesn't make sense to Hire Smart People and tell them what to do. We hire Smart People so that they can tell us what to do "

— Steve Jobs—

Being selected for an interview is a significant milestone in your journey. It reflects the progress you've already made and your potential. Now, it's time to trust in yourself, your story, and your abilities. The steps you've taken so far have prepared you to confidently present your best self and showcase your unique talents to the world.

At the end of this Chapter, you will be able to;

- Why companies use interviews to hire people?
- What to expect from different types of interviews?
- What should you do before and after the interview.
- How do you face the interview confidently

Why Companies Use Interviews

Interviews are a critical part of the recruitment process because they provide insights that a CV or cover letter cannot fully capture.

They help employers assess:

- Candidate's Fit for the Role and Organisation

    Person, Position and Personality Match: As Chapter 2 highlighted the Career Defining triangle, Interviews allow employers to evaluate the candidate's professional background and how their skills align with the job requirements. They also reveal the candidate's personality, which is essential for cultural fit. Interviews test the candidate's comprehension of the job responsibilities and their alignment with the organisation's mission, values, and culture.

    - **Motivations and Contributions**: Employers can explore why the candidate applied for the job, what drives them, and how they plan to add value to the organisation. They also uncover any potential concerns about the candidate's skills or abilities and provide an opportunity for clarification.

    - **Alignment with company value and Culture**: A wise man once said that the words people use can shape a culture. Therefore, it is important to reflect on personal values, attitudes, and beliefs to ensure they align well with the existing company culture.

- Soft Skills and Behavioural Traits
    - **Teamwork and Collaboration**: Employers look for indicators of whether the candidate can work effectively in teams. Assessment Centres, Case-based interviews and Competency-based interviews used to evaluate these.
    - **Emotional Intelligence and Motivation**: Interviews assess the candidate's ability to handle challenges, communicate effectively, and stay motivated.
    - **Potential Value**: Employers evaluate how the candidate might contribute to innovation, efficiency, and a positive work environment.

- Track Record of Impact
    - Employers seek specific examples of achievements, problem-solving capabilities, and measurable outcomes from the candidate's previous roles.

Types of Interviews

Interviews are designed to assess a candidate's suitability for a role by evaluating their skills, experience, behaviour, and cultural fit. Interviews come in various formats, each with a unique focus, setting, and set of expectations. While you might know the type of interview in advance, that's not always the case. Familiarizing yourself with the most common types will help you prepare effectively and approach any interview with confidence.

Below is an overview of common interview types, when they are used, what they measure, and preparation tips.

Face to Face Interviews

Face-to-face interviews are commonly conducted for roles that involve customer interactions, especially in the later stages of the hiring process, where personal connections or cultural fit are evaluated. These interviews often assess communication skills, professional demeanour, and overall alignment with the organisation. In smaller companies, these interviews may be one-on-one with the director or conducted as a panel, with participants from different areas of the business involved in the decision-making process.

Having been involved in interviewing candidates at both entry and experienced levels, I've often been surprised by how unprepared some young candidates are.

Reflecting on my own experience, I've faced many panel interviews while progressing through my career both in Sri Lanka and in the UK. One key takeaway is that, regardless of the position, what truly matters is what you bring to the table and your ability to articulate it well. It's essential to research the company and the role thoroughly, practice answering common interview questions, dress appropriately, and maintain good body language. Additionally, preparing thoughtful questions for the interviewer is crucial. When you're aware of the panel members, or at least their roles, make sure to address each person, maintain eye contact, and project strong body language to make a lasting first impression. It's also helpful to study their LinkedIn profiles, blog posts or read any articles they've published, as referencing these during the interview shows your preparation and eagerness.

Phone Interview

Phone interviews are often used as an initial screening step to narrow down candidates. The goal is to assess basic qualifications, interest in the role, communication skills, and visa status, among other factors. It's important to schedule the phone interview carefully. If you receive an unexpected call from the company and are not in a quiet environment, politely ask for a few minutes to find a private space or request to reschedule for a more convenient time.

Always have your CV and the job description on hand. Be prepared with a concise personal overview or elevator pitch that you can share when needed. Listen attentively and avoid interrupting the interviewer. If a question is unclear, ask them to repeat it to ensure you understand and can provide an accurate response.

Your voice can reflect your personality, and the background noise in your environment can leave an impression as well. How you handle the call, including your greetings, demonstrates your interpersonal skills. Treat every interview opportunity with equal importance, regardless of the format, to make a positive impression.

Video Interview

Video interviews can feel unfamiliar, but with the right preparation, they provide an excellent opportunity to showcase your skills and personality. As remote work becomes more common,

video interviews are increasingly used to streamline the hiring process and reduce resource utilization. While this can sometimes be challenging due to technology, it's also an opportunity to demonstrate your digital proficiency.

The most important factors for success are having a stable internet connection and a well-lit room. Always log in from a laptop in a professional setting with a clean, neutral background. Avoid attending an interview while travelling, as this can give the impression that you are unprepared and not prioritizing the interview.

While casual dress is common for many remote jobs, especially in technical fields, there's nothing to lose by presenting yourself in a more professional manner. Start by making a strong first impression, dress appropriately, ensure your setup is tidy and well-lit, and test your technology in advance to avoid any glitches.

During the interview, focus on being authentic and fully engaged. Maintain eye contact by looking at the camera, silence notifications, and ensure you're not interrupted. While having your CV and keynotes nearby is helpful, avoid relying too heavily on them. Practice your responses to common questions to stay confident and composed.

Treat a video interview with the same level of professionalism as an in-person one. By preparing thoroughly, staying focused, and adapting to the video format, you'll set yourself up for success and leave a positive impression.

Competency-Based Interview

Competency-based interviews provide hiring managers with a structured and reliable method to evaluate candidates by focusing on their skills, abilities, experiences, and knowledge. These interviews operate on the premise that past behaviour is a strong indicator of future performance. As such, questions typically emphasise transferable skills such as communication, adaptability, and resilience, often beginning with prompts like *"Give an example of," "Describe how you,"* or *"Tell me about a time when."*. Most often the employers give details about the interviews and sample questions to ready before the interview. By looking at it you can identify that this will be a competency-based interview.

Here's how you can effectively prepare for a competency-based interview:

To prepare, review the job description to identify key competencies and align your responses with the language and values of the company. Gather specific examples demonstrating these skills from work, academics, volunteering, or extracurricular activities, ensuring authenticity and relevance. Use the STARR technique (Situation, Task, Action, Result, Reflection) to structure your answers and make them impactful. You will explore more on this later in this chapter. Practice answering common questions through mock interviews or self-recordings to build confidence and improve delivery, helping you present your abilities effectively.

Technical Interviews

A technical interview is designed to evaluate your technical knowledge and expertise, often including problem-solving tasks or practical tests. These interviews are common in fields such as engineering, IT, data science, and other technical roles. Questions will typically relate to your educational background, professional experience, and the specific technical skills required for the position.

If the role involves creative or technical work, you may be asked to bring a portfolio showcasing previous projects. Be prepared to explain your approach, methodologies, and the decision-making processes behind your work.

To succeed in a technical interview, consider the following tips:
- Review key concepts and technical knowledge relevant to the role.
- Practice solving problems or coding challenges to sharpen your problem-solving abilities.
- Be ready to clearly explain your thought process, especially when solving complex problems.
- Stay calm and take time to think through each question, demonstrating both technical expertise and a logical, structured approach.

By preparing thoroughly and focusing on both your technical skills and ability to articulate your process, you'll make a strong impression in a technical interview.

Case Interview

Case interviews, commonly used in consulting and other strategic roles, are designed to assess your critical thinking, problem-solving abilities, and analytical skills. During a case interview, you'll be presented with a hypothetical business problem and asked to analyse and solve it. The case may involve elements such as strategy, market analysis, calculations, or observations.

To excel in a case interview, follow these steps:

- **Clarify the problem**: Ensure you understand the case thoroughly by asking clarifying questions before diving into your analysis.
- **Structure your approach**: Break down the problem into manageable parts and outline a clear framework for tackling it.
- **Think aloud**: Share your thought process with the interviewer. This demonstrates your ability to approach problems logically and analytically.
- **Use data effectively**: If provided with numbers or data, incorporate them into your analysis to support your conclusions.
- **Stay focused:** Keep your solution relevant to the problem at hand and avoid overcomplicating the issue.

A successful case interview shows not only your ability to solve problems but also your approach to tackling complex challenges with clarity and structure.

Assessment Centres

Assessment centres are commonly used for graduate schemes, managerial roles, or positions that require a diverse set of skills. These evaluations assess multiple competencies, including teamwork, problem-solving, leadership, and adaptability. During the assessment, you may participate in various exercises such as role-plays, presentations, and group tasks designed to test your ability to collaborate, communicate, and perform under pressure.

To succeed in an assessment centre, it's important to understand the structure and nature of the exercises beforehand, and practice relevant skills such as psychometric tests and group interactions. Focus on both individual tasks and group activities, ensuring you contribute effectively while remaining adaptable and calm throughout. Most importantly, be yourself and give your best effort, do not try to outdo others but instead focus on demonstrating your unique strengths and abilities.

Presentation Interview

This format is often part of an assessment centre or a final-stage interview. In this scenario, you'll be assigned a topic to present to key stakeholders, allowing you to demonstrate your communication, analytical, and problem-solving skills. The topic could be work-related or more general, but it should showcase your ability to think critically and present complex ideas clearly and concisely.

To make your presentation stand out, consider using the "10-20-30 rule": no more than 10 slides, a total presentation time of no longer than 20 minutes, and a font size of at least 30 for readability. Presenting in a professional manner, keeping it simple and focused, will help you engage your audience effectively.

Additionally, practice until you can present smoothly and confidently. Practising in front of a mirror can help you fine-tune your delivery and make a significant difference in your overall performance.

10 Tips to Prepare for the Interview

Securing an interview is a great achievement. Congratulations! Now, it's time to prepare so you can really impress. A little preparation goes a long way in helping you stay confident and perform at your best.

Once Your Interview is Confirmed:

Tip 01 - Research the Organisation

You've likely done some research when submitting your application, but now is the time to dive deeper. What are their current projects? Have they been in the news lately? Who are their clients? Knowing this will help you engage with the interviewers and demonstrate your genuine interest in the company. If you know who will be interviewing you, researching their LinkedIn profile or any articles they've published can help you connect with them and reduce any nervousness.

"Once, someone I interviewed had pulled out quotes from journalists about the company, and I was so impressed. It showed how much effort she'd put in and how much she cared about the organisation." – Director, Events Business.

Tip 2 - Prepare for Common Questions

Review the job description and the skills required for the role. This will give you a sense of the questions you're likely to face. Make a list of possible questions and think through your answers. Don't feel pressured to fit into a perfect answer; let your personality and experience shine. You can also use tools like Virtual Interview Practice to rehearse responses.

Remember, interviews are as much about your personality as your qualifications. Don't hesitate to mention personal projects or hobbies that are relevant to the role. These will show the interviewer why you're a good fit.

Tip 03 - Research Career Progression and Training Opportunities

It's important to consider how the role fits within the team or company. Research the potential career paths available within the organisation. This will show you're thinking long-term and genuinely interested in growing with the company. If relevant, consider mentioning any courses or qualifications that would enhance your skills for the role, but avoid focusing too much on this during the interview.

Tip 04 - Arrange Any Extra Support You Might Need

Now workplace is evolving as Inclusive. If you require special accommodations for your interview, don't hesitate to reach out to the organisation beforehand. This could include adjusting the interview room, providing materials in alternative formats, or arranging for an interpreter or other support.

Tip 05 - Plan Your Route

Ensure you know the exact location and how to get there. Use online tools to find the best route and add extra time to avoid arriving stressed or late.

Tip 06 - Decide What to Wear

Don't leave outfit decisions to the last minute. Plan what you're going to wear a few days in advance so you can focus on the interview itself. Check out resources for tips on what to wear to an interview and feel confident in your attire. Select your "Power Dress".

A Few Days Before:

Tip 07- Prepare Your Own Questions

During your research, you'll likely come across questions you want to ask the interviewer. Write them down so you're ready when they ask if you have any questions. Check out our guide for top questions to ask in an interview.

Tip 08 - Practice with Friends or Family

Rehearsing with someone else can help ease your nerves and make you more comfortable during the interview. Have a friend, family member, or mentor conduct a mock interview to help you practice.

The Day Before:

Tip 09 - Review Your Notes

Take a moment to go over the notes you've prepared. Familiarize yourself with your responses to potential questions, but don't try to memorize everything. A good grasp of key points will help you sound natural and confident during the interview.

Tip 10 - Get a Good Night's Sleep

A restful night's sleep is crucial. If you're tired during the interview, it will show. Being well-rested will help you stay focused, confident, and alert, making it easier to handle any unexpected questions.

"It's noticeable when an interviewee hasn't had enough sleep. They seem less focused, and it doesn't leave a good impression." – Head of HR, Marketing Agency

Every interview is different, and sometimes, you may have less time to prepare. These steps can be condensed depending on your situation. However, the key is to ensure you walk into the interview feeling calm, confident, and ready to present the best version of best version of yourself. Good luck for your interview.

Facing the Interview

Congratulations! You've already cleared several hurdles to get to this stage, proving you're one of the best candidates. Your chances of success are strong, over 50%! The rest depends on how well you perform during the interview.

It's essential to remember that each company has its own unique recruitment process, often tailored to the specific job role. This means you may encounter various types of interviews or assessments during the process. While this guide provides general scenarios, the tools and tips shared here can help you approach any interview with confidence.

You're ready. All you need to do is stay calm, professional, sensible, and focused. **You've got this!**
Now, let's explore some critical tools and tips to ace your interview.

The Three Touch Points
An interview doesn't begin when you sit at the table; it starts the moment you set foot in the organisation. Keeping the **Three Touch Points** approach in mind will help you make an excellent impression throughout the process.

1. The reception
- Arrive early and introduce yourself to the receptionist with a pleasant demeanour.
- Many companies observe candidates' behaviour even before the formal interview. Reception staff may share feedback on how well you interact, so treat this as your **first touch point.**

2. The Waiting Area

- While waiting, you may encounter other visitors, fellow candidates, or even company employees. Any of these individuals might assess you informally.
- Early in my career, I would engage with candidates in the waiting area to observe their attitudes and behaviour before the formal interview began. Treat these interactions as your **second touch point.**

3. Casual Encounters

- Whether it's a quick chat in the lobby, a trip to the restroom, or walking to the interview room with a company representative, these moments matter.
- For example, if the director's assistant escorts you, use this time to create a great impression. Be polite, confident, and professional—this can serve as your **third touch point.**

4. Refreshments

- If offered tea or coffee, accept it graciously and handle the situation with poise. Demonstrating good etiquette can further solidify a positive impression.
- Throughout the process, maintain positive gestures, proper posture, and an approachable attitude. These small details contribute to your overall impression.

5. The Formal Interview

Once you're at the interview table, the focus shifts to how you communicate and present yourself. Whether it's a competency test, video interview, panel discussion, or face-to-face interaction:

- **Listen attentively:** Make sure you understand each question before answering.
- **Stay focused:** Respond to the point with clear, concise answers.

- **Use positive body language:** Confident gestures and a professional posture convey self-assurance.
- **Create a strong impression:** Engage with enthusiasm and showcase your unique strengths.

6. Wrapping Up the Interview

Even after the interview concludes, you're still being observed.

- Maintain good eye contact and thank the interviewers sincerely.
- Walk confidently as you leave, demonstrating composure and positivity.
- Don't forget to thank the receptionist on your way out, leaving a final positive impression.

If you successfully navigate at least three touch points, starting from your arrival to the conclusion of the interview, you significantly increase your chances of success. Each interaction is an opportunity to reinforce your professionalism, adaptability, and readiness for the role.

Now, let's dive deeper into specific interview questions and strategies in the next section. You're on your way to acing this interview. Good luck!

The Key to Success

Effective Communication is the key to success in an interview both Verbal and nonverbal. Everyday conversations can sometimes leave us puzzled. What is the speaker's true intention? Often, meetings end with an overload or a lack of information, making it hard to retain the critical points. This underscores the power of communication, shaping how others perceive and remember you.

Communication is not just about words. Stanford psychologist Nalini Ambady's research highlights this brilliantly. In her study, students watched 5-6 seconds video clips of lecturers they had never met and rated them on personality traits such as confidence, competence, and approachability. Remarkably, these snap judgments aligned closely with evaluations from students who attended full lectures. This demonstrates how quickly we form opinions about others. As an early-career professional, understanding this can transform how you approach crucial moments, such as interviews, whether on the phone, online, or face-to-face. Research reveals that it will take less than 11 seconds to create a first impression. (You will also learn about 4 step frameworks in creating a lasting impression in Chapter 8).

To create a lasting impression:

1. **Clarity of Intent**: Know the key message you want to convey.
2. **Non-Verbal Cues**: Consider posture, tone, and facial expressions. They speak volumes.
3. **Practice**: Rehearse, delivering your message concisely and confidently

In today's fast-paced world, intentional communication isn't just a skill; it's your superpower. How you present yourself in those critical first moments can define how you are remembered.

Body language is a powerful way to communicate feelings through gestures, posture, and facial expressions. Whether intentional or not, interviewers often make assumptions based on your nonverbal cues.

For instance, crossing your arms might be interpreted as defensiveness. By becoming more aware of your body language, you can take control of the impression you leave during an interview.

Certain habits are commonly seen as signs of engagement and can make a strong impression, such as:

- **Making regular eye contact**
- **Maintaining an upright, confident posture**
- **Smiling naturally**
- **Nodding to show attentiveness**

Displaying these behaviours can help convey confidence and enthusiasm.

If you're neurodivergent and find some of these habits challenging, don't feel pressured to conform to traditional expectations. Recruitment practices are increasingly inclusive, and many employers strive to accommodate diverse communication styles. If you're comfortable, consider disclosing your neurodivergence early in the process to prevent misinterpretation of your body language. However, this is a personal choice, and there's no right or wrong answer.

Relaxation Is Key!

Ultimately, the best impression comes from being relaxed. When you feel calm, it sets a positive tone and boosts your confidence.

Here are some ways to reduce pre-interview nerves:

- Practice **calming breathing exercises** to centre yourself.
- Listen to **uplifting music** or an empowering podcast.
- Explore and incorporate techniques that work for you, such as mindfulness or Visualisation.

Preparation Builds Confidence

Thorough preparation can also help ease anxiety. Knowing your skills, understanding the company and role, and anticipating the interview format allows you to focus on presenting your best self.

- Research the role and company in depth.
- Practice common interview questions or arrange a mock interview with a friend or online tool.

Be Authentic

Above all, be yourself. Interviews are stressful enough without the added pressure of pretending to be someone you're not. Authenticity allows your personality to shine and helps the interviewer connect with the real person behind the CV.

By blending self-awareness, preparation, and authenticity, you'll leave a memorable and positive impression, setting yourself up for success.

Types of Interview Questions

We can allocate all the interviews into four categories.

1. **Questions about you**
2. **Job- Specific**
3. **Employer-Specific**
4. **Competency based**

Let's explore more about each category in detail.

About You

By now, your CV has already provided a substantial overview of your qualifications, skills, and experience. However, interviews go beyond the written word. They offer a chance to see the person behind the document. Employers want to observe how you articulate your thoughts, present yourself, and demonstrate your personality. Your presence and the way you communicate tell a story that can't be captured on paper.

When discussing yourself, it's essential to focus on alignment on how the responsibilities of the role match your skills, personality, and aspirations. This is the essence of the *Career Defining Triangle* discussed in Chapter 2. Reflect on how your strengths connect with the role and how your personality complements the demands of the position.

Authenticity and honesty are critical. Your words, actions, and demeanour must align. Any inconsistency or hint of dishonesty can immediately raise doubts and jeopardise your chances. When answering "Tell me about yourself" or similar questions, stay genuine and grounded.

Speak with conviction, highlighting your journey, motivations, and the unique value you bring to the role.

Remember, your goal is to leave an impression of consistency and credibility, showing them you're not just qualified but also a perfect fit for the organisation's culture and needs.

When preparing for interview questions, it's crucial to draw inspiration from examples while maintaining your authentic voice. Your unique way of communicating, rooted in your experiences, personality, and insights, will set you apart. The proposed approaches and examples below provide a framework, but how you articulate your answers should reflect your individual style and genuine self.

Proposed approach with some common examples

1. What is your biggest strength?

Proposed Approach:
- Identify a strength that reflects your gifts, passions, and expertise (as discussed in Chapter 2's *Career Defining Triangle*).
- Connect it to the job requirements.
- Use personal examples to explain why it's a strength and how it will benefit the role.

Example:
"One of my biggest strengths is strategic thinking, which I honed during my years managing brand innovation for Brazil and Latin America. I can take a high-level challenge, break it down into actionable strategies, and execute with precision. For this role, I'll use this skill to identify growth opportunities and drive impactful results."

2. What is your biggest weakness?

Proposed Approach:
- Be honest and self-aware.
- Share the actions you've taken to overcome the weakness and how it has shaped you.

Example:
"I used to struggle with public speaking, finding it nerve-wracking to address large audiences. Realizing the importance of this skill, I joined Toastmasters and started practising regularly. Now, I not only feel confident presenting but also enjoy engaging audiences, a skill I've applied while teaching and delivering workshops."

3. Why are you looking for this job?

Proposed Approach:
- Tie the role to your professional aspirations and values.
- Reference specific company initiatives, values, or achievements that resonate with you.

Example:
"I'm excited about this role because it combines my passion for growth strategy with the opportunity to contribute to a company known for its innovative approach. Your recent wellbeing initiative reflects values I deeply believe in, and I see this position as a chance to build on my skills while aligning with an organisation that prioritizes people and purpose."

4. What are your career goals for the next 5 years?

Proposed Approach:
- Share a clear and ambitious goal that aligns with the company's vision.
- Make it more realistic and not show ambition. Your aim is to secure the job.
- Explain the steps you're taking toward achieving it.

Example:
"In the next five years, I aim to lead transformative projects that drive growth for global organisations. I've already taken steps, such as designing leadership workshops and gaining cross-functional experience, which have prepared me to take on strategic roles like this one."

5. What motivates or stresses you?

Proposed Approach:
- Explain what drives your passion and productivity.
- Share how you've learned to handle stress constructively.

Example (Motivation):
"I'm motivated by challenges that push me to think creatively and solve problems. For example, leading the development of the Employability Certification Program showed me the satisfaction of creating impactful solutions that help others succeed."

Example (Stress):
"I used to feel stressed by last-minute changes, but I've learned to manage them by staying flexible and focusing on the bigger picture. Now, I view change as an opportunity to adapt and innovate."

6. What hobbies do you have?

Proposed Approach:
- Connect hobbies to transferable skills or qualities that enhance your professional capabilities.

Example:
"I enjoy writing, and I'm currently working on my book, Essential Complete Guide for Early Career Professionals. This hobby sharpens my ability to communicate ideas clearly and connect with diverse audiences, skills that directly benefit my professional roles."

7. If you were an animal, what type of animal would you be?

Proposed Approach:
- Use this metaphor to highlight your personality and values.
- Tie it back to qualities relevant to the role.

Example:
"I'd be a honeybee, focused, collaborative, and productive. Honeybees work tirelessly for the collective good, which mirrors my own approach to teamwork and achieving shared goals. Like them, I bring energy and purpose to every project I take on."

While these examples provide inspiration, your success lies in adapting them to your own experiences, voice, and style. Authenticity is powerful; embrace it in your conversations to leave a lasting impression.

Job Specific

Interviewers ask job-specific questions to gauge whether you have the skills, knowledge, and experience required for the position. Even for entry-level roles, your ability to study the job description, Visualise the responsibilities, and tailor your responses is crucial. For experienced positions, you must also demonstrate how your expertise aligns with the role's challenges and goals.

Let's explore how to approach these questions effectively, with examples tailored for early-career professionals and experienced job seekers.

1. Why should we hire you to do this job?

Approach:
- For early-career professionals: Focus on your enthusiasm, learning agility, and alignment with the job requirements.
- For experienced professionals: Highlight your proven track record and how your specific skills match the role's needs.

Example (Early-Career Professional):
*"I'm a quick learner with a solid foundation in **[specific skill or knowledge area, e.g., digital marketing]**. I've gained hands-on experience through projects during my degree, such as **[specific project]**. I'm eager to bring fresh ideas and energy to your team and contribute to your goals."*

Example (Experienced Professional):
"With over eight years of experience in strategic marketing and business growth, I've successfully led projects that delivered [specific achievement]. My skills in [key skills] align perfectly with your current needs, and I'm confident I can contribute to achieving [specific goal or challenge mentioned in the job description]."

2. **Why do you want this job?**

Approach:
- Show enthusiasm for the role, relate it to your career aspirations, and demonstrate knowledge of the company.

Example (Early-Career Professional):
"I'm excited about this opportunity because it allows me to apply my skills in [specific area] and develop new ones in a dynamic environment. Your company's commitment to [specific value, e.g., innovation or sustainability] inspires me, and I see this role as a perfect start to building a meaningful career."

Example (Experienced Professional):
"This role aligns with my passion for driving growth and innovation. I admire your company's achievements in [specific area] and see this position as an opportunity to leverage my experience in [specific skill/area] to contribute to your continued success."

3. What particularly interests you about this job?

Approach:
- Identify a specific aspect of the role that excites you, such as the scope, challenges, or learning opportunities.

Example (Early-Career Professional):
*"I'm particularly excited about the opportunity to work on **[specific responsibility]** because it aligns with my passion for **[specific field]**. I look forward to learning from your team and contributing to **[specific company** goal]."*

Example (Experienced Professional):
*"I'm drawn to the strategic aspects of this role, particularly **[specific responsibility or project]**. It's an area where I've made significant impact before, and I'm eager to bring that expertise to your team."*

4. Tell me about your previous experience in a similar job/industry.

Approach:
- Share relevant examples of tasks or projects that relate to the role, focusing on achievements and transferable skills.

Example (Early-Career Professional):
*"While I'm new to the industry, I've gained relevant experience through **[internships/projects]**. For example, during my internship at **[company]**, I worked on **[specific task]**, which helped me develop skills in **[key skills]**."*

This is where you bring your transferable skills into discussion (Refer to Chapter 03)

Example (Experienced Professional):
*"In my previous role as **[position]** at **[company]**, I successfully **[specific achievement]**. This experience has equipped me with **[key skills]** that I can apply effectively in this role."*

5. **What would be your greatest challenge in doing this job?**

Approach:
- Acknowledge a potential challenge honestly but show how you plan to address it.

Example (Early-Career Professional):
"As a recent graduate, I expect the initial challenge to be understanding your processes and tools. However, I'm confident that my eagerness to learn and adaptability will help me overcome this quickly."

Example (Experienced Professional):
"The greatest challenge might be getting up to speed with your unique systems and processes. However, I have a track record of quickly adapting to new environments and delivering results."

6. **What would you find easy about this job?**

Approach:
- Highlight areas where you already have expertise and can add value immediately.

Example (Early-Career Professional):
"I'd find it easy to adapt to the collaborative aspects of this role. I've always thrived in team settings, contributing ideas and supporting peers to achieve goals."

Example (Experienced Professional):
"I'd find it easy to manage the strategic planning aspect of the job. It's an area where I have extensive experience, having successfully driven [specific achievement]."

7. What would be your dream job?

Approach:
- Relate your dream job to the role, showing alignment with your aspirations.

Example (Early-Career Professional):
"My dream job is one where I can continuously learn and grow while contributing to impactful projects. This role feels like the perfect step toward that vision."

Example (Experienced Professional):
"My dream job involves leading transformative initiatives in [specific field], which aligns closely with the scope of this role and your company's mission."

8. What would you do in your first 30/60/90 days in this role?

Approach:
- Demonstrate your proactive mindset and understanding of the role.

Example (Early-Career Professional):
"In the first 30 days, I'd focus on learning your processes, building relationships with the team, and understanding expectations. By 60 days, I'd start contributing to projects and implementing my skills. By 90 days, I'd aim to deliver measurable results and provide insights to improve workflows."

Example (Experienced Professional):

"In the first 30 days, I'd immerse myself in understanding the company's culture, team dynamics, and current challenges. By 60 days, I'd implement strategies to address key objectives. By 90 days, I'd aim to deliver results, such as [specific goal or milestone], and contribute to long-term planning."

Pro Tips:
- Research the Role Thoroughly: Study the job description to Visualise the role and its scope.
- Practice Your Answers: Rehearse responses to ensure clarity and confidence.
- Be Authentic: Tailor answers to your experiences and strengths while aligning with the role.
- Use the STAR Method: For example, structure responses around *Situation, Task, Action, and Result. You can explore more in the next section.*

Whether you're just starting your career or advancing to a senior role, preparation and authenticity will ensure you shine during job-specific interviews.

Employer-Specific Insights

You wouldn't walk into a stranger's house uninvited, would you? Similarly, employers expect you to do your homework and research the company before stepping into an interview. Why? Because it shows your genuine interest in the job and reflects your attitude toward the opportunity.

Think about it, your job is where you'll spend most of your waking hours. It should be fulfilling, exciting, and aligned with your values. The company culture must suit your needs as much as you suit theirs.

In the UK, **Glassdoor** is a fantastic resource for understanding the company from an employee's perspective. It gives you a behind-the-scenes view of what it's like to work there. Another great resource is their **website**, which provides everything from their mission statement to the latest news.

You can also **talk to people in your network** or, better yet, find someone working at the company. They might give you first-hand insights about the work environment. Some companies even offer office visits for candidates preparing for presentations or specific projects.

Don't forget platforms like **LinkedIn**, **indeed**, **Trustpilot**, and **Google Reviews**. These are treasure troves of information about how the company interacts with its community, clients, and employees.

Now, let's dive into some examples of employer-specific interview questions and how you can tackle them with confidence.

Common Questions and How to Approach Them

1. What do you know about us?

This is your moment to show that you've done your research. Talk about:

- How you first came across the company (e.g., through a friend, an article, or social media).
- Three things you admire about them. Be specific, whether it's their innovative products, values, or CSR initiatives.
- If appropriate, mention one area where they could improve and offer a suggestion. This shows initiative and critical thinking.

Example Response:

"I first learned about your company through a LinkedIn post celebrating your recent innovation in renewable energy. What really stood out to me was your commitment to sustainability, the way you prioritize employee development, and your excellent reputation for customer service. One thing I noticed is that your website could highlight your recent achievements more prominently. It's a great story worth sharing!"

2. What is your favourite type of working environment?

Think about what you've learned about the company culture and align your response with it. Be honest about what motivates you, but ensure it fits the role.

Example Response:

"I thrive in collaborative environments where innovation and teamwork are encouraged. From what I've read about your company, I see you value these qualities, which makes me confident this would be an ideal workplace for me."

3. What can you bring to our company?

This is where you highlight your strengths and back them up with evidence using the **STAR** method. Align your answer with the company's goals or projects.

Example Response:

"In my previous role, I led a cross-functional team to implement a new customer feedback system. We comprehensively studied the existing system and industry best practices and came up with a new Customer Feedback management system which linked to individual performance evaluations of the employers. This resulted in a 25% improvement in satisfaction scores within

six months. Therefore, I'm confident that my ability to identify gaps and implement solutions aligns with your focus on continuous improvement."

4. Tell me, what you think about our products and services.?

If possible, experience the product or service yourself before the interview. Alternatively, gather opinions from your network to provide an authentic answer.

Example Response:
*"I've been a user of your **[product/service]** and have always appreciated its reliability and ease of use. Additionally, I've spoken to a colleague who uses your service regularly, and they were particularly impressed with your customer support. It's clear you prioritize quality and customer satisfaction."*

5. What do you know about our competitors?

This question tests both your industry knowledge and your ability to evaluate the company objectively. Be honest, but always emphasise what makes this company stand out.

Example Response:
*"I've researched your competitors, such as **[competitor name]**, and noticed they focus heavily on cost leadership. However, what sets you apart is your emphasis on quality and customer loyalty. Your recent campaigns around sustainability are particularly impressive and resonate with me personally."*

6. What would you like to know about us?

This is your chance to show curiosity and genuine interest. Prepare thoughtful questions that reflect critical thinking.

Example Questions:
- *"How does the company plan to achieve its long-term goals, and how does this role contribute?"*
- *"Can you tell me more about the team I'll be working with?"*
- *"What do you enjoy most about working here?"*

The key to nailing employer-specific questions is preparation. Research, practice, and genuine curiosity will set you apart from other candidates. When you approach these questions, remember to:

- Be specific and authentic.
- Align your responses with the company's goals and culture.
- Showcase your skills and how they contribute to the company's success.

The effort you put into understanding the company will not only help you stand out but also ensure that you're stepping into a role where you can truly thrive.

Competency Based

This is, ideally, a STARR Battle. Employer will evaluate how competent you are in handling particular situations, such as leading a team, Handling a difficult conversation, working under pressure, etc. As an early career professional, you can narrate your hobbies, School, university or charity work to explain transferable skills and personal attitudes that will highlight a situation.

Let's explore some questions.
1. Tell me about a time when you demonstrated good leadership Skills?
2. Tell me a time that you handle a Difficult customer?
3. Tell me about a time when you handle a Crucial Project?
4. Tell me about a project that you deliver as a team?
5. Tell me about a time you worked under pressure and how you managed it?

Study the below technique and try answering the above questions.

STARR Technique

Answering interview questions effectively can be daunting, especially when you're put on the spot. The STARR technique offers a clear framework to help you deliver strong, structured, and impactful responses that showcase your skills and experience.

S: Situation
Begin by setting the scene.

- What was the context?
- Who was involved?
- What was happening?

Keep your explanation concise and relevant to the skill or experience the interviewer wants to learn about. For instance, if asked to demonstrate leadership, you might say:

"I was part of a busy team tasked with producing monthly financial reports under very tight deadlines."

T: Task
Clarify the specific challenge or objective you faced.
- What needed to be done?
- What role did you play?

Describe this succinctly, such as:

"I noticed a new team member was overwhelmed, which jeopardized the timely completion of their section of the report. I decided to step in and support them."

A: Action

This is the crux of your answer. Detail the steps you took to address the task.

- What actions did you take?
- Why did you choose this approach?
- How did you execute it?

Focus on your contribution:

"I initiated an informal conversation to understand their struggles. They shared their difficulties with the reporting software, so I offered to provide one-on-one training. For a week, I met with them daily, guided them through the software, and answered their questions."

R: Result

Highlight the tangible outcomes of your actions.

- What did you achieve?
- What was the impact on the team, project, or organisation?

Be specific and measurable where possible:

"As a result, they completed their reports on time and to a high standard. By their next performance review, they were surpassing their targets."

Normally, we use the STAR technique which is most prominent in the context. However, you can add another pro tip to elevate your STAR.

Pro -Tip

R: Reflection

(Optional but impactful) Share what you learned or how the experience influenced your professional growth.

- What insights did you gain?
- How has it shaped your approach since?

Add a reflective note:

"This experience not only helped the new hire succeed but also revealed my passion for training others. Since then, I've actively taken on mentoring roles."

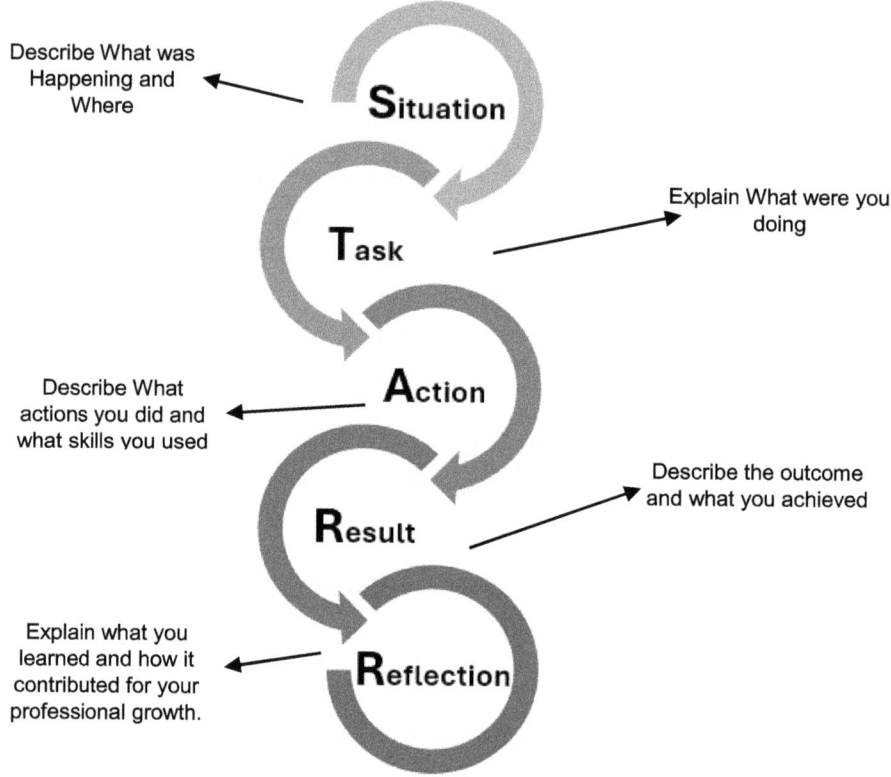

Describe What was Happening and Where → **S**ituation

Explain What were you doing →

Task

Describe What actions you did and what skills you used ← **A**ction

Describe the outcome and what you achieved

Result

Explain what you learned and how it contributed for your professional growth. ← **R**eflection

Figure 15 - STARR Technique Outline

Practice Makes Perfect

Try using the STARR framework with a friend or mentor. Have them ask you situational questions, and craft your responses using this structure. With practice, you'll build confidence and ensure your answers leave a lasting impression.

Try applying the STARR method for the questions below and practice.

- Can you describe an activity or project where you had to take responsibility?
- What are you most proud of that you have worked on in school/college/in a part-time or volunteering role?
- Can you tell us about one of your biggest achievements?
- Describe a time when you've had to deal with a difficult situation?
- Tell me about a time when you tried something in a different way to get the result you wanted?

After the Interview

For many, the post-interview phase is simply a waiting game. You wait for the employer to contact you, deliver their decision, positive or negative, and then move on. But is there anything you can do during this period to minimize your chances of rejection? The answer is 'yes'.

After interviewing HR specialists and asking them, *"How many candidates follow up after an interview?"* the response was striking. Very few do. When I followed up with, *"Does following up negatively influence your decision?"* the unanimous answer was, *"Not at all! In fact, we love to see enthusiasm."*

Their insights revealed that candidates who follow up often leave a stronger impression. Even if they don't get the current role, they are remembered for future opportunities. Some HR professionals even forward these candidates to upcoming vacancies. A follow-up demonstrates initiative, gratitude, and genuine interest, all traits employers value.

Being called for an interview is already a testament to your qualifications. If you don't get selected, it doesn't mean you're not good enough. It simply means that the competition was stiff, and only a limited number of positions were available. Use rejection as a stepping stone, not a stopping point.

The Importance of Follow-Up

After the interview, take these key steps to stay proactive:
1. **Send a Thank-You Email**
   Within 24 hours of the interview, send a concise email thanking the interviewer(s) for their time and the opportunity. This small gesture can make a big impact.

Use this opportunity to express gratitude and reinforce your interest in the role.

Example:

Subject: Thank You for the Opportunity

Dear [Interviewer's Name],

Thank you for taking the time to interview me for the [Job Title] position at [Company Name]. I truly appreciated the chance to learn more about your team and the exciting projects you're working on. I am genuinely enthusiastic about the opportunity to contribute my skills to your organisation. Please let me know if there's any additional information I can provide.

Best regards,

[Your Name]

2. **Request Feedback**

   If you don't get selected, ask for feedback in a professional manner. This helps you understand areas for improvement and shows that you're focused on growth.

   Example:

   Thank you for considering my application for the [Job Title] position. I was wondering if you could share any feedback from the interview that could help me improve. I greatly appreciate your insights.

3. **Follow Up After a Few Days**

   If you haven't received any response after 5–8 working days, send a polite follow-up email. Avoid coming across as desperate. Instead, focus on reiterating your interest in the role and seeking an update on the hiring process.

Example:
Subject: Follow-Up on Interview for [Job Title]
Dear [Interviewer's Name],
I hope this email finds you well. I wanted to kindly follow up on the status of my application for the [Job Title] position. I remain very enthusiastic about the opportunity to join [Company Name] and contribute to your team. Please let me know if there's any update you can share. Thank you again for your time and consideration.
Best regards,
[Your Name]

Rejection can be a powerful learning tool. Use any feedback you receive to refine your skills, improve your interview techniques, and strengthen your candidacy for future opportunities. Review the strategies and examples from Chapter 6 to leave a lasting impression in subsequent interviews.

By following these steps, you can set yourself apart from other candidates and turn the post-interview phase into a strategic advantage. Even if you don't land the job, you've laid the groundwork for future opportunities.

In summary

Mistakes That Can Ruin Your Interview (And How to Avoid Them)
Navigating the interview process can be challenging. Mistakes can happen not only during the interview but also before and after. Here are some common pitfalls and tips to help you steer clear of them:

1. Failing to Research the Role
If you don't show a solid understanding of the role or company, the hiring manager might assume you're not genuinely interested. Take time to study the job description, company website, and social media channels to gain insights and tailor your approach.

2. Overlooking Your Own Skills and Experience
Don't just read the job description—reflect on how your skills align with the key requirements. Think of concrete examples that demonstrate your strengths and how you've applied them successfully in past roles.

3. Skipping Practice
Confidence is key, and practice is the best way to build it. Conduct a mock interview with a friend, practice in front of a mirror, or use an interview simulator. Research common questions and rehearse your answers to prepare for different scenarios.

4. Ignoring Dress Code Expectations
Your attire matters. If you're unsure of the dress code, opt for something slightly formal. Ensure you're clean and presentable—coffee stains or messy hair can distract from your professionalism.

5. Arriving Late

Punctuality makes a strong first impression. Plan to arrive early to account for delays. For remote interviews, log in a few minutes ahead of time to check your technology and settle in.

6. Displaying Impoliteness

Politeness goes beyond the interviewer—it extends to everyone you interact with. Listen actively, avoid interrupting, and show engagement by nodding or summarizing questions in your answers.

7. Dwelling on Negatives

If discussing challenging past experiences, focus on how you managed or learned from them. Avoid blaming others or speaking negatively about previous employers—it can come across as unprofessional.

8. Failing to Ask Questions

Asking thoughtful questions shows your interest in the role and company. Prepare a few in advance, and jot down any that arise during the interview to demonstrate curiosity and engagement.

9. Skipping the Follow-Up

After the interview, send a thank-you email within 24 hours. Express gratitude, reiterate your enthusiasm for the role, and remind the interviewer why you're a great fit.

Final Tip: Preparation is your ally. Research, reflect, and practice to ensure you're putting your best foot forward. And don't forget to set your alarm—being late could undo all your hard work!

08

Thriving in your New Role

After years of hard work and unwavering dedication ; facing rejections, overcoming challenges, and navigating the complexities of a VUCA world; you have fortified your core and successfully broken into the world of work. Now, you stand at the threshold of a new role, ready to embark on an exciting chapter in your life.

At the end of reading this Chapter, you will be able to,

- Identify 7 important aspects that you need to consider when evaluating a job offer.
- Compare a given offer with your needs.
- Identify Effective ways of negotiating and communicating with your employer.
- Discover important tips for winning your first day at work
- Develop 30-60-90-day plan to thrive in your role.

Settling into a job can feel like finding the right relationship. Sometimes, you strike gold with your first love and commit to life. Other times, it may take several attempts, filled with disappointments and setbacks, before discovering the right match. The journey of finding a job is no less intricate. It requires careful consideration of your best career fit based on your skills, values, and aspirations. Balancing multiple priorities and opportunities is an ongoing challenge. Importantly, this journey isn't solely about money.

Opportunities don't come by mere "luck." I believe **LUCK = PLAN × OPPORTUNITY.** By aligning your plans with available opportunities, you create your pathway to success.

Imagine that you got your new offer which is the gateway to your success. Here is a framework to analyse the job offer before deciding.

The 7 P Framework

1. Place

Consider the job's location. Is it at the headquarters or a branch? Evaluate the cost and time involved in commuting or travelling. Does the role require flexibility, such as hybrid work arrangements or international travel? Understanding these factors helps you assess how well the job aligns with your lifestyle and financial priorities.

2. People

Life is shaped by the people we meet and the experiences we create with them. Your workplace is no different. Consider the team, their backgrounds, and cultural dynamics. Is the workplace diverse? Will you interact with young students, experienced professionals, or corporate executives? Understanding these dynamics is vital in assessing the interpersonal value of your job.

3. Price

While salary is a critical factor, it's essential to acknowledge the **law of diminishing returns**—where excessive wealth doesn't necessarily increase happiness. Human desires evolve, and satisfaction levels shift with income growth. Evaluate the offered salary against industry standards and consider how it supports your lifestyle.

4. Passion and Purpose

Reflect on what excites you to wake up and work. This is your **passion**. The Japanese concept of **Ikigai** beautifully captures the intersection of passion, mission, vocation, and profession.

Figure 16 - Concept of IKIGAI

Align your job with what you love, what you are good at, what the world needs, and what you can be paid for. For instance, a teacher who loves working with children, excels at it, and earns recognition and income from this passion finds purpose in their work. Does your prospective job align with these principles?

5. Progress

Smaller organisations often provide broader responsibilities, offering significant learning opportunities, though compensation might be modest. In contrast, larger corporations may offer better packages but with narrowly defined roles. Consider the company's structure, flat or hierarchical, and explore horizontal and vertical growth opportunities. Networking with current employees or alumni can provide valuable insights into growth prospects.

6. Policies

Every organisation has unique policies and ethical guidelines. For example, bankers may face restrictions regarding side jobs, while medical professionals adhere to stringent work ethics. Additionally, contractual commitments, work hours, and regional regulations may influence your decision. Ensure the company's policies align with your personal and professional needs.

7. Priorities

Your priorities define the significance of job elements, such as flexibility, salary, or work-life balance. What percentage of importance would you assign to each? For example, does the role offer the flexibility to support family commitments? Or does it provide the network and skills necessary to start your own business in the future? These considerations ensure the job supports your long-term goals and satisfaction.

Before deciding, reflect on your **priorities**, which vary by individual, age, and circumstances. How much weight would you assign to different aspects of your life? Clarifying this can be instrumental when evaluating job offers and career decisions.

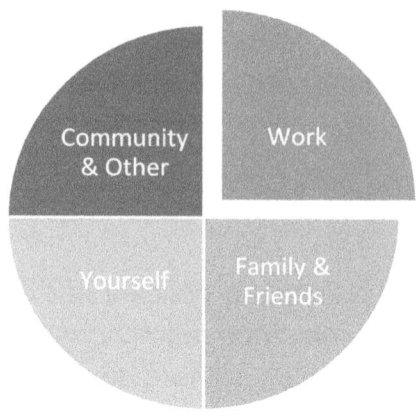

Evaluate your job offer holistically by considering these aspects, balancing tangible benefits like salary with intangible ones like purpose and growth. When you align a role with your values and goals, you're more likely to find long-term satisfaction and success.

Offer and Needs

You've invested significant time and effort into gathering knowledge, studying the job market, learning new skills, crafting your CV, and applying for jobs that align with your aspirations. This journey likely involved sacrifices and dedication. But have you taken a moment to assess your market value and how you measure it?

Sabri Suby's book *Sell Like Crazy* offers an insightful perspective on valuing your time. In many Asian contexts, time is often offered generously to family, friends, and work without considering its monetary worth. In contrast, Western cultures tend to place high value on every hour. Reflecting on your worth means acknowledging the time and effort you've invested in your journey and the skills you bring to the table. This self-awareness can significantly enhance your ability to negotiate and evaluate your job offer.

Understanding Your Needs Before Accepting an Offer

Before you accept a job offer, it's essential to identify your priorities. Ask yourself:
- What do I truly need from this job?
- Is my primary goal financial stability, career growth, or both?
- Will this role enhance my profile by associating me with a reputed company?

Additionally, consider the specific benefits the job provides:
- Does it include international travel or opportunities to work globally?
- Are the working hours flexible, or will they require extended commitments?

- Does the position offer logistical convenience or flexibility that outweighs monetary benefits?
- Will the role help develop your skills and network, potentially paving the way for future entrepreneurial ventures?

Understanding your needs will help you make a more informed decision and evaluate whether the offer aligns with your personal and professional goals.

Comparing and Researching the Job Offer

Once you've outlined your needs, compare the offer against industry standards and competitor packages. Look into what other companies offer for similar roles, including additional benefits such as:

- Travel or vehicle allowances.
- Insurance coverage.
- Increment policies.

This research will help you gauge whether the offer is competitive and prevent future dissatisfaction. Consulting someone in the field can also provide valuable insights, helping you avoid surprises after accepting the job. Feeling undervalued or overworked from day one can led to dissatisfaction and hinder your performance.

Balancing Lifestyle and Financial Expectations

Your lifestyle is another critical factor to consider. Young professionals today often have different lifestyle expectations compared to previous generations. Reflect on the minimum income required to sustain your current lifestyle comfortably.

For example, during my early career, I vividly recall struggling to manage my first salary. I often found myself relying on my parents by the end of the month, which raised questions about my negotiation skills at the time. Learning from such experiences can guide you to avoid similar situations.

Evaluating the Offer Details

When reviewing your job offer, focus on the details:
- **Basic Salary:** Ensure it covers your minimum lifestyle costs. Remember, bonuses and commissions may vary and are often influenced by external business factors.
- **Allowances and Benefits:** Assess the value of allowances such as mobile, travel, or health insurance. While these perks are valuable, your basic salary is the foundation for your financial stability.

By conducting thorough research and evaluating the offer holistically, you can confidently decide whether it meets your needs. A well-informed decision sets the stage for a fulfilling work experience and ensures you won't feel undervalued or regretful later.

Negotiating your Offer

When you receive a job offer, it often starts as a **Conditional Job Offer (CJO)**. This document outlines the terms of employment, allowing you to review critical details such as salary, working hours, retirement benefits, additional responsibilities, reporting lines, job duties, probationary period, and any conditions you must fulfil during the probation. Employers usually give you 5–10 working days to respond, which is an ideal window to negotiate if you've already analysed your needs and market rates.

Platforms like **Glassdoor** are excellent resources for exploring employer reviews and gaining insight into compensation and benefits packages, especially if you're in Europe. Reviewing this information equips you with the knowledge to make informed decisions and negotiate effectively.

Negotiation: A Positive Opportunity

Employers value professionalism during negotiations and generally view it as a positive attribute. When I received my first job offer at a bank; one of the top five employers at the time, I noticed the basic salary was like other offers. However, the additional benefits and the moral satisfaction derived from the company's culture and values aligned closely with my degree. With advice from the Head of HR, I made the choice after careful consideration, and it proved to be the right one.

Similarly, during my placement selection, all options were in rural branches. To make an informed decision, I visited these branches as a customer to silently observe their work environments. This helped me gain clarity on my choice.

Communicating Your Counteroffer

Once you've reviewed the offer, it's essential to communicate your perspective thoughtfully. Always send your response in writing, expressing gratitude for the opportunity while logically presenting up to four key points for consideration. Here's an example:

Sample Counteroffer Email

Subject: Review of Job Offer

Dear [Hiring Manager's Name],

Thank you for offering me the position of [Job Title] and for taking the time to provide feedback. I deeply appreciate the opportunity and am excited about the possibility of contributing to [Company Name].

After carefully reviewing the offer, I would like to share my perspective on a few aspects of the terms:

1. While the performance allowance is attractive, the basic salary of [current offer] falls below the industry average as per my research. I would feel more comfortable and aligned with a basic salary of [proposed amount], which meets my financial needs and expectations.
2. Regarding the 40-hour workweek, I have personal commitments requiring me to travel home on Fridays. I kindly request consideration for reduced hours on Fridays, aligning with a 37-hour workweek.
3. For the notice period in case of voluntary resignation, I would prefer a one-month notice period instead of the stated two months for better flexibility.

I've made these requests with the intention of contributing my best to the role, ensuring a mutually beneficial arrangement. I look forward to hearing your thoughts and am open to discussing further.
Kind regards,
[Your Full Name]

The Zone of Possible Agreement (ZOPA)

During negotiations, both parties typically find a middle ground, often referred to as the **Zone of Possible Agreement (ZOPA)**. Employers aim to retain promising candidates, so a reasonable counteroffer often leads to a revised agreement.

Once the final offer is ready, most companies today provide a digital version to sign or, occasionally, a physical letter to sign and return. Be sure to keep a copy of the final agreement for your records.

By approaching this process with research, professionalism, and clear communication, you can ensure that the offer aligns with your needs and career goals, setting the stage for a fulfilling role.

Master your First Day

The Day You've Been Waiting for Is Here – Make It Count!

The day you've been preparing for has finally arrived. You are ready to shine and make an impact. Before stepping into it, take a moment to Visualise your success. I remember a story shared by Nilantha Malagamuwa, the renowned racing car champion, at a conference.

He said,

"Before every race, I close my eyes for five seconds and visualise myself celebrating victory. I immerse myself in that feeling, which helps me focus my thoughts and perform at my best."

This practice is powerful and can be applied to your first day as well. Spend a few minutes Visualising your success and how you will thrive, excel, and make a lasting impression. Remember, the key to success lies in how you present your authentic self.

Presenting Your best self

Your first impression sets the tone for how others will perceive you. It's essential to be intentional in the way you present yourself. Here is a memorable framework for you to follow.

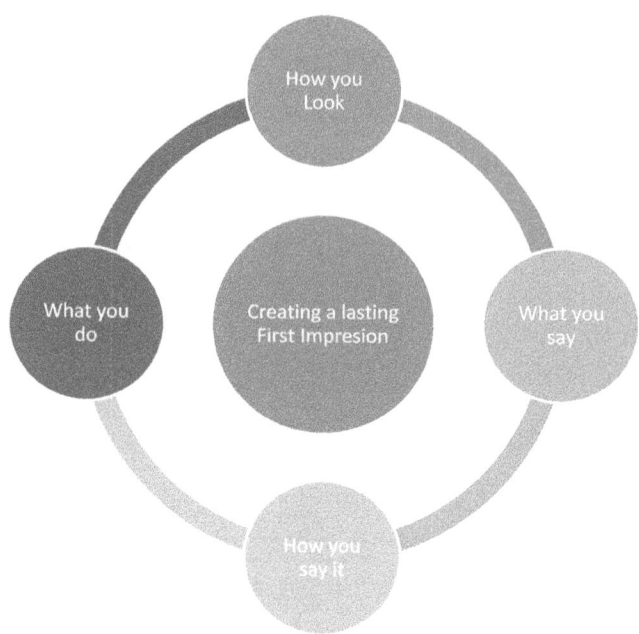

Figure 17 - 4 step framework for creating a lasting first impression

How you look

Your attire adds value to your presence and creates an identity for you. Mastering the art of selecting the right outfit; one that suits your body type, complements your complexion, and aligns with the occasion; requires practice and experimentation. Workplace attire often varies based on organizational culture, so it's essential to understand and adapt to these norms.

For your first day, aim for a smart, formal look that aligns with the company's style. Reflect on what you observed during your interview, and if possible, confirm expectations with your contacts to avoid overdressing or underdressing. Choose colours that enhance your appearance and ensure your outfit and shoes are well-coordinated. Subtle, professional makeup and grooming contribute to a polished and appropriate look.

Dressing well not only helps you appear professional but also boosts your confidence. Consistency in your style is key; avoid creating a standard of dress that you cannot maintain over time. Wearing clean, well-balanced attire that aligns with your personality will help you gradually build your personal brand in the workplace.

Remember, it's not just about your clothes; your makeup, hairstyle, and accessories also play an important role. If you're unsure about what's appropriate, don't hesitate to ask your contacts for guidance before your first day.

What you Say

What you communicate; verbally, nonverbally, and in written form; shapes the first impression you create. This process begins from the very first interaction with the company. Avoid using slang, focus on speaking concisely, and tailor your communication to suit your audience. Listening actively and responding professionally with well-thought-out sentences is crucial.

Workplaces thrive on effective conversations but navigating them thoughtfully is essential. Refrain from gossiping and keep discussions professional and respectful. Neutral topics like hobbies, travel, or sports can be excellent conversation starters, especially when building rapport.

Focus on listening attentively rather than simply waiting for your turn to speak. Asking open-ended questions, such as "What motivates you here?" encourages meaningful dialogue. As John Lee emphasizes with the acronym *REAL*:
- **Reach out** to initiate connections.
- **Engage** by acknowledging others and asking thoughtful questions.
- **Ask** questions that make others feel comfortable.
- **Listen** with genuine interest.

During your initial days, prioritize listening and observing the workplace culture before sharing your opinions. Avoid dominating conversations or overly promoting yourself, as this can come across as boastful. By being mindful of your communication, you'll build strong, positive relationships and create a lasting impression.

How you Say it

Equally important is ensuring your body language aligns with your message. Use open gestures, practice appropriate handshakes, and work on establishing genuine connections with people. It is also important to add confidence into your tone.

Confidence begins with how you feel about yourself. Your demeanour plays a vital role in how others perceive you. Start with a genuine smile. It's magnetic and shows approachability.

Maintain eye contact by focusing on the area between the eyebrows, which strikes a balance between confidence and comfort.
When offering a handshake, ensure it is firm and warm, with a maximum of three shakes parallel to your body. Stand tall and walk with your back straight and your head held high. Slow, deep breaths will help you stay calm and composed. Together, these actions project confidence and poise.

What you do

Your first day is an excellent opportunity to establish meaningful connections. Plan who to meet, where, and when. Follow the instructions provided to avoid confusion.
Familiarize yourself with key contacts, including your supervisor, team members, and colleagues. Understand your

manager's expectations rather than making assumptions; roles and responsibilities can differ significantly between organisations. Take the time to clarify any uncertainties about your job description.

Every workplace operates differently. Spend your first day observing team dynamics and understanding the organisational culture. Learn how your role contributes to the team and identify key interdependencies.

Avoid stepping on toes by being overly assertive, but also ensure you don't remain invisible. Strike a balance by participating where necessary while focusing on learning and adapting to the environment.

Your induction is a critical time to familiarize yourself with HR systems, reporting structures, key performance indicators, and workplace policies. Use this time to get your IT setup and logistics in order, ensuring a smooth start to your role.

Be mindful of workplace politics. Identify toxic individuals and maintain a professional distance from them. Instead, align yourself with colleagues who share your values and have a positive outlook. When addressing challenges, avoid asking your manager what to do; instead, present potential solutions and seek their feedback. This demonstrates initiative and problem-solving skills.

Consistency in your behaviour from day one is vital for building trust and credibility. Maintaining a professional and reliable demeanour ensures that your first impression lasts.

Consider finding a mentor within the organisation who can offer guidance and feedback. A mentor can help you understand how others perceive you and provide valuable advice on navigating workplace dynamics.

Respect for diversity is also crucial in today's workplace. Understanding generational and cultural differences will help you thrive in a multicultural environment. For instance, direct communication styles from Eastern cultures may seem blunt, while British politeness may mask disagreement. Adapt to these nuances to build strong relationships.

Your first day is a significant milestone. By dressing appropriately, building confidence, fostering meaningful connections, and observing workplace culture, you set the stage for long-term success. Present your authentic self, stay consistent in your actions, and take pride in creating a positive and lasting impression.

30-60-90 days Plan

As highlighted in Chapter 7 on interview questions, employers often ask about your 30-60-90-day plan to assess how you envision contributing to their business. This chapter provides clear insights and actionable tips to create an effective plan that sets you apart from other candidates.

Employers hire you because they believe in your potential to contribute to their goals. While **early career professionals** may feel uncertain about crafting such a plan, taking the initiative to create one demonstrates foresight and preparation.

Detailed job descriptions offer valuable insights into what the role entails. Additionally, asking clarifying questions during the interview can help you understand the company's expectations better. With this knowledge, you can craft a personalized 30-60-90-day plan that aligns with the organisation and showcases your readiness to contribute.

Step 1: The First 30 Days – Learning and Adjusting

The initial 30 days are about onboarding, learning the ropes, and settling into your new role. This is your opportunity to understand the organisation, its processes, and its culture. Some goals to consider include:

- Completing all required HR training sessions.
- Meeting co-workers and relevant stakeholders; setting up regular meetings to build rapport.
- Working with your assigned buddy to familiarize yourself with internal processes.
- Reading circulars, process documents, and project plans to gain insights into ongoing initiatives.
- Scheduling a one-on-one meeting with your manager to gather feedback and align expectations.

Your primary focus during this phase is observation, adaptation, and gaining clarity about your responsibilities.

Step 2: The Next 60 Days – Contributing and Building Confidence

By the second month, you'll have a better understanding of your role and the organisation, enabling you to contribute effectively while requiring less guidance. Some potential targets include:

- Achieving small, measurable wins to showcase your strengths.
    - For instance, completing five successful sales calls, reviewing a process, or conducting initial interviews.
- Seeking feedback from co-workers or your supervisor to refine your performance.

- Completing a relevant certification or training course that enhances your skills and productivity.

At this stage, your focus shifts from learning to demonstrating your ability to add value and integrate seamlessly into the team.

Step 3: The Final 30 Days – Driving Results and Initiatives

By the end of 90 days, you should be working independently, initiating improvements, and contributing to long-term goals. Use this phase to build on what you've learned and deliver meaningful outcomes. Some objectives might include:

- Proposing a new project idea or suggesting improvements to existing processes.
- Reflecting on your first 90 days and drafting a comprehensive plan for the rest of the year.

- Meeting with your manager to review your performance, gather feedback, and discuss future goals.

This phase focuses on consolidating your role and demonstrating initiative, creativity, and leadership potential.

Your 30-60-90-day plan doesn't need to be extravagant. It should be realistic, with SMART goals. Additionally, include ways to track and evaluate your success. As part of your interview preparation, you'll already be researching the company, the role, and its responsibilities. Use this understanding to craft goals that reflect your ability to adapt quickly, contribute effectively, and align with the organisation's vision. By presenting a well-thought-out plan during the interview, you'll showcase your readiness to hit the ground running and make an immediate impact.

Stay Relevant

The workplace is a VUCA world. In this AI-driven and cyber-centric era, it is constantly evolving. Thriving in a career requires continuous improvement of your skills and knowledge to stay relevant. Equally important is strengthening your mental and physical well-being to face these challenges.

Resilience is a critical skill that we must master at every stage of life. Janet Marshal, a leading talent management professional, shared a fascinating analogy about resilience during a recent discussion. She compared resilience to the characteristics of an oak tree and a willow tree during a storm. While the oak tree is strong, it may not withstand the storm as well as the flexible willow tree, which bends and adapts to the winds, ultimately surviving the crisis. This highlights an important lesson: being strong is not enough; the ability to be flexible and adaptive in challenging situations is even more crucial.

Figure 18 - Resilience of a Oak and Willow tree

Another essential component of building resilience is developing emotional intelligence; the ability to perceive, understand, and manage your own emotions while navigating relationships effectively. Emotional intelligence is especially important when working in teams, as it fosters collaboration, empathy, and effective communication.

By cultivating resilience and emotional intelligence, you can not only thrive in your career but also lead a more balanced and fulfilling life. These qualities will empower you to adapt to change, overcome obstacles, and succeed in an ever-evolving world.

In Summary

- It is important to analyse your offer and negotiate benefits that align with your lifestyle to build a fulfilling career. The 7P framework provides guidance for organizing this analysis.

- Communication with your employer should be clear, concise, and professional. Ensure your requests are reasonably justified and supported by valid arguments. Use the provided sample communication template to assist you.

- Creating a lasting first impression is not just about your first day; it lays a solid foundation for the future. Maintaining consistency and staying true to your personal identity are crucial. Use the 4-step framework to thoughtfully plan your day.

- Having a **30-60-90-day** plan for your career sets the tone for your performance and demonstrates to your line management that you are working with a clear strategy.

- Building resilience and emotional intelligence are crucial skills for navigating your career and achieving a fulfilling life.

Conclusion

As you prepare to embark on this transformative journey into the world of work, envision yourself as a seed, firmly planted in the dynamic soil of a VUCA world; volatile, uncertain, complex, and ambiguous. Through adaptability, self-awareness, and goal setting, you have nurtured your potential, equipped with the tools, techniques, and knowledge to thrive not just in your first job but throughout your career. These skills will serve as your foundation, guiding you step by step as you navigate the career ladder. With every milestone, the experiences you gain, the people you meet, and the wisdom you acquire will propel you to the next level.

Remember, goals are fluid, they evolve with you. Make time to reflect on your journey, recalibrate your aspirations, and embrace growth. Success lies in seizing the right opportunities and mastering the art of aligning them with your goals.

In this new phase of your life, you need a reliable compass to steer you toward success. From my own experiences, and through the insights gleaned from countless accomplished individuals, I've developed what I call the "success compass." This compass is not just a tool; it's a mindset, a transformative force that aligns your direction with your highest potential.

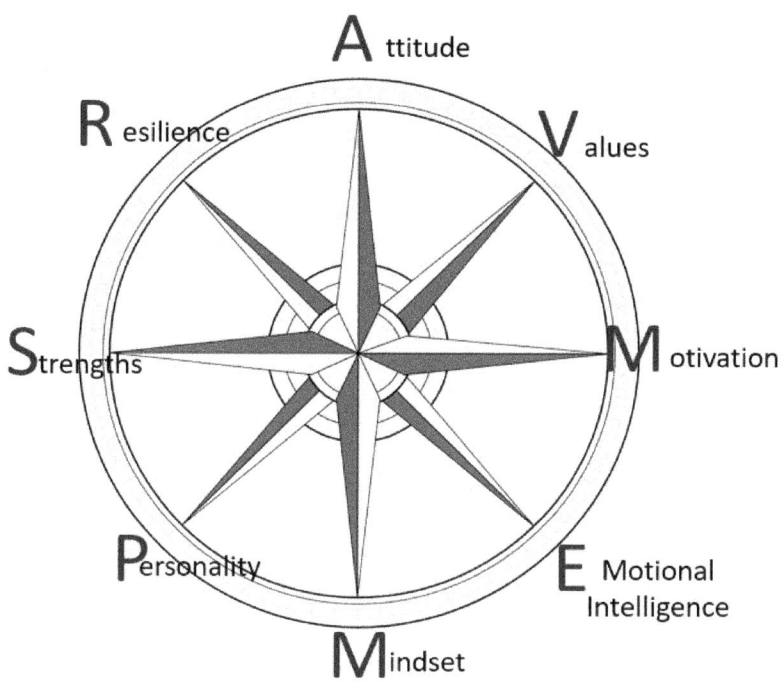

Copyright @ipcd Sucesscompass

Figure 19-The success Compass

*Here's how it works: when you surround yourself with the right environment and the right people, your beliefs and behaviours shift positively. This will shape your **Attitude**. It leads to a growth **mindset**, opening doors to new learning and honing your **strengths**. When you use your Strength, **Motivation** flows naturally, driving you to explore opportunities and acquire knowledge that shapes your core **values**. Living by these values refines your **personality**, crafts your unique identity, and inspires others to follow your lead. As you inspire, you'll build **resilience**, fearlessness, and positivity; qualities that will set you apart. Engaging with society enriches your understanding of both you and the world, sharpening your **emotional intelligence** and reinforcing your ability to navigate life's complexities. The more you align with this compass, the closer you'll move toward enduring success.*

So, as you step forward, keep expanding your knowledge, have unwavering faith in yourself, and focus on what truly matters. Direct your energy toward things you can control and trust the journey. With determination and persistence, you'll not only break into the world of work—you'll thrive and make a meaningful impact.

It's time to embrace your potential. Let's start **Breaking In** and begin this exciting chapter.

Final Note

If you believe this book can add value to someone's life, please consider leaving an Amazon review or gifting a copy to someone who might benefit from it. Your support can make a meaningful difference, and I'm sure they will be truly grateful.

www.ingramcontent.com/pod-product-compliance
Ingram Content Group UK Ltd.
Pitfield, Milton Keynes, MK11 3LW, UK
UKHW021508110325
456069UK00006B/500